Life Lessons

Life Lessons

A Purpose-Driven Leadership Journey

Alison Browne-Ellis

*"When I think about how far I have come, given where I started,
I feel compelled to share some important life lessons."*

Table of Contents

Acknowledgments · ix
About the Author · xi
Preface · xiii
Introduction ·xvii

Understanding Your Purpose ·1
Attitude Is Everything ·6
Get Up, Get Dressed, and Show Up! ·11
Consider Your Game Plan ·14
Personal Branding Is Real ·19
The Growth Factor ·24
Growth and Gratitude ·29
The Power of Discipline ·33
Embracing Accountability ·36
Managing Risks ·39
Overcoming Obstacles ·43
Building Capacity ·47
Feedback as a Recipe for Success ·51
Claim Your Seat at the Table ·55
Stay Committed to Helping Others Grow · · · · · · · · · · · · · · · · ·59

From a Leader's Perspective ·63
Leadership Requires Continuous Learning · · · · · · · · · · · · · ·66
Leading in Times of Crisis ·70
The Balancing Act ·75
Embrace the Journey ·79
Conclusion ·83

Life Lessons Summary· ·87

Acknowledgments

"In all things, I give God thanks!"

The daily struggles I witnessed growing up with my mum gave birth to the dreams and vision I had for my life, along with the acknowledgment that anything worth having, comes with some degree of personal sacrifice. From as early as I can remember, I knew that in order to own my dream for a different life, I needed to adopt the same values of hard work, determination, and perseverance that I saw in both my mum and grandmother, and I needed to do so consistently. This book is dedicated to my Grandmother Thelma, who was my biggest fan, and to my mum Marcia, my very best friend! My hope is that the life lessons shared in my book will inspire my daughter Amyah and my nieces and nephews: Tamme, Tamika, Shaquam, Dakaria, Sha-Neil, Demario, Torey, and Darielle, who now have their whole lives ahead of them, in addition to anyone seeking to embark on a rewarding professional career journey.

I also wish to thank all my professional mentors who provided such invaluable guidance throughout my progressive career, along with my avid supporters, whom I sometimes feel believed in me more than I believed in myself.

About the Author

As a Caribbean girl from the beautiful island of Barbados, Alison Browne-Ellis is proud to carry the label of a strong, black, independent, successful, and transformational leader. *Life Lessons: A Purpose-Driven Leadership Journey* speaks to dreams, struggles, and success. Alison Browne-Ellis strongly believes that the personal struggles presented in her childhood have uniquely shaped her leadership style and career journey. By no means a stranger to hard work, she lives by two core philosophies: *"anything worth doing, simply needs to get done,"* and *"you have to love what you do."* These personal philosophies have guided her work ethic over the years and helped her to successfully build a strong personal brand.

Today, Alison Browne-Ellis has overcome struggles of all magnitudes as she quickly made her way up the corporate ladder. Now seen as a change agent and transformational leader, Alison Browne-Ellis has over twenty-two years of experience within the financial services industry where she has gained the respect of the local business community and many across the Latin America Caribbean region. She holds an Executive Leadership Diploma from the Ivey Business School, Western University and an MBA with Distinction from the University of Surrey. She is also an Affiliate Member of the Chartered Institute of Marketers and has served as an Executive and Council Member for the Barbados Chamber of Commerce and Industry. Her passion for mentoring and coaching others has also led to her completion of the John Maxwell Team Certification.

As a mother of a beautiful and talented twelve-year-old daughter and professional mentor to many, Alison hopes that she can continue to inspire the values of hard work, determination, discipline, and remaining true to self, which have brought her to this point in her professional journey. The burning desire and passion for mentoring others remains at the forefront of her mind, giving birth to this collation of important life lessons now shared in the following pages of her book.

Alison Browne-Ellis would be the first to admit that she is by no means a writer; however, having always been led by her strong spiritual faith, she believes that any seed planted by God possesses the ability to be fulfilled.

Preface

I remember laying on the couch at my friend Sarah's new apartment during my first Christmas in Canada, staring at the fireplace and trying feverishly to shake off that burning desire to begin writing my life's story and get back to some much-needed sleep. A memory flashed across my mind of this frail-looking little girl with really short, reddish-brown hair that stuck out everywhere; she was so skinny with a broad face that sheepishly lacked confidence. I recall smiling broadly and feeling a sense of sheer satisfaction, as thankfully, I was not that frail little girl anymore and highly doubt that anyone would ever use those words to describe me. Yet, my hesitation to entertain the thought of even writing the book took me down a completely different path at two in the morning.

The memories of my childhood are quite clear; I believe I could have been five at the time but could have easily passed for three years old because of my frail build. I loved dolls even though I can't remember ever owning a brand new one. Wherever my mum got our secondhand clothing and toys from, I guess they knew I loved dolls too. I was just so grateful, because only now I realize that I lived the dreams and fantasies that gave me hope through my secondhand doll collection. As a little girl, my mum used to work at Intel, an offshore firm that made machine parts, so she used to work quite a bit of night shifts. With no father around, I was left at the mercy of my two older brothers and sister, and boy was that a traumatic experience at times. I used to always question if they loved or even liked each other, because the house always felt like a war zone. As my sister suggests up to this day, I always seemed to be the center of the controversy that caused my siblings to go at each other like cats and dogs. In hindsight, I think they were mean to each other under the guise of protecting me from one another. Nights were always a battle zone, yet my mum somehow managed to bring about order in the morning, which usually saw me hiding in a corner and peeping over at my siblings, who were generally either missing in action or weeping in a corner of our one-bedroom chattel house. Ironically, my sister, who was undoubtedly very mean to me at home, was also my biggest defender in public. Kids hesitated to call me names whenever my sister was around as she would go after them with a vengeance. This always puzzled me, since I quietly saw her as the meanest of them all.

At 2:35 a.m., those memories threw me in a spiral, which meant that getting back to sleep was surely out of the question. My thoughts continued to wander, and this strong urge to write and share my life lessons with others somehow remained at the surface, consuming my mind. I was no writer! Why was this burning desire to write constantly on my mind? Where would I even begin, I wondered? Between my work schedule and other demands, I was often faced with the trap of being too busy, which at times causes me to shift into autopilot. So again, I asked myself, when would I ever find the time? Maybe I was going through some kind of midlife crisis as I was approaching forty in another month. All I knew was that I just could not shake this feeling. The urge to share my life story was way too important to ignore and at that very moment I knew that God was yet again directing my journey, which meant that I would absolutely need to find the time to share these important life lessons.

In her book *Becoming*, Michelle Obama talks about the power of using your authentic voice and sharing your truth even though it isn't always easy. Truthfully, over time I have been moved emotionally by the positive impact I have had on others by allowing myself to be known and heard both in my personal and professional space. My passion for connecting and engaging with other professionals is very much driven by a burning desire to reach back and help others. The more I thought about how far I had come, given where I started, I felt compelled to share my life lessons as I am constantly reminded that "to whom much is given, much is expected!" *Life Lessons: A Purpose-Driven Leadership Journey* is just another way for me to fulfill my God-given purpose in such a way that extends a helping hand to others.

This collection of life lessons that offer practical career experiences highlights the personal qualities, skills, tools and techniques needed for success from a leader's perspective. My hope is that this book can act as a roadmap or guide for other aspiring leaders seeking to navigate the challenges of career advancement and leadership, while building a strong personal brand. It is important to note however, that the author strongly believes that leaders do not need to have a fancy title; they can simply have the ability to positively influence others while creating traction that supports both personal and professional advancement.

Introduction

*"To get something you never had, you have to do
something you never did!"*

—Denzel Washington

W hen and how did I get here? Hard to believe that I am raising a daughter who's so confident and assertive, with a wit about her, a corny sense of humor, and an even more peculiar sense of style. What's more! Here I am today, a corporate executive very much at the forefront of transformation at a highly respected and well-established organization. Truth be told, for many years, I never really took time to reflect on my professional journey. I was always so focused on the next goal, the next project, or reaching the next level that I aspired to, that looking back was not something I often practiced. As I was approaching my fortieth birthday, I found myself somewhat emotional, overwhelmingly so at times. Allowing myself the time to pause, reflect, and acknowledge all that I had accomplished, considering where I had come from, and oh, what a journey it has been!

I must admit upfront, starting from humble beginnings really has been the underlying driver of my passion, discipline, and determination over the years. Growing up, I saw my mum fight day in and day out to create a better life for our family. I remember how the pain and agony that was so visible on her face as she returned home in the evenings, used to hurt me so deeply. From a tender age, this undesirable pain caused me to make a silent promise to myself that I would never allow her efforts to go in vain. I was always to remain grounded and thankful for what little we had, never envying others but more so, allowing their blessings to be an inspiration for me to seek a better life; believing that if they had it, I could work to achieve the same. I vowed to go after a life that did not exist in my family's inner circle and to break the cycle of poverty that was so prevalent all around me. I can say without a doubt that today, I am truly satisfied with all that I have achieved, and the and the ceilings' successfully broken! A story that I am no longer hesitant or afraid to share because it a hundred percent defines who I am today—as a mother, daughter, wife, friend, mentor, and business leader.

I do appreciate that we all define success differently! For some, it's that big house and nice car. For others, it's that prestigious career and fancy title. For me, success is all about finding that place of peace I have been searching for all my life and the recognition that I am now able to sustain a certain quality of life, while being a true inspiration to others. Not sure why but my fortieth birthday brought about this feeling of contentment and sheer satisfaction. With this feeling of peace over my life, I was truly at a place where I was so focused on how I can help others to achieve their own personal dreams and professional goals. Michelle Obama reminds us that "when you've worked hard and done well and walked through the door of opportunity, do not slam it shut behind you; reach back and give others the same chances that helped you to succeed."

From the way I am constantly trying to encourage and inspire others, to the values I am working daily to instill in my daughter, to the love and care I have for my family and friends and even for complete strangers, I feel a sense of accomplishment in helping others. Furthermore, what is heartening is the approach I take to manage through the rigors of business, while focusing on building strong relationships in order to achieve organizational goals. These traits collectively encompass who I am. And, I somehow think for the first time that I was prepared to accept that this has always been a part of my life's purpose. I am a package and part of that package includes my past; a past filled with important defining moments that can offer guidance to other future leaders and young professionals seeking to climb the corporate ladder; and even for other professionals at the pinnacle of their careers, yet fail to achieve the ability to connect with others.

The practice of self-reflection is obviously a good thing because it highlighted to me the importance of the "power of pause." Truthfully, I don't even know when this happened, but in that moment I realized that I absolutely love the person I had become! Ultimately, this is what has led me here, and my only hope is that the life lessons shared throughout this book can cause you too to reflect on your own personal and professional journey, while inspiring thought-provoking moments that help you to embrace the journey ahead.

Understanding Your Purpose

"Failure will never overtake me if my determination
to succeed is strong enough."

—Og Mandino

Teenage years are always the hardest and, for me, these really were the most defining years of my life. The struggles of growing up with a single mum intensified because many of my high school activities had to be prioritized. For the most part, I did not have the luxury of attending such activities unless they were mandatory or carried a clear benefit to my academic performance.

Purpose Is Rooted in Defining Moments

Ironically, part of the parenting arrangement my mum and father put in place was for him to deliver my weekly allowance to my Secondary School on Mondays. Imagine, most weeks, the Wednesday would have come and passed, and my father would still

Alison Browne-Ellis

be a no show. In an attempt to protect my mum from any additional and undue stress, I always defaulted to struggling through those days without lunch, unless one of my kind-hearted schoolmates offered to share with me and, in extreme cases, lend me bus fare until my father decided to grace me with his presence. I will not lie to you that that was a real rough patch, yet I can safely say that being in the situation fueled the determination and passion that so many people see in me today.

By the end of my third year, when we were selecting our career subjects, I recommitted a promise to myself that I would buckle down and be the one in my family to break this prevailing cycle of poverty. I realized that if I was going to do better, I had to do more, so I put together a plan and started putting in some real work. At thirteen years old, I had determined that this approach was going to shape my entire outlook on life and would lead me into a position where I would never have to depend on anyone financially ever again. Being in a position to bring my mum into a new way of living was also extremely high on my agenda. I often reminisced about the vision I had for our lives since I desperately needed the pain and worry I saw in her face to disappear permanently.

I was quietly determined to make something of myself, and nothing within my control was going to stop me. I was going to stand out on the merit of my attitude, always putting in tremendous effort and going the extra mile. I never really aimed to be the best, only the best that I could be. The vision I had for our lives saw us overcoming the financial struggles and enjoying a new quality of life. My efforts started to be validated by all my high school teachers, whose constant sentiments included, "Alison tries really hard." Over time, my mum became so proud and, for once, I was able to see a spark of hope and pride in her that I had never seen before. She started to believe in me, and it felt good; together,

2

we began to see a brighter future ahead, and I was excited to be leading the way.

This desire to break the cycle of poverty in my family gave me an inner drive that I seem incapable of dialing back, even today, despite all my progress. I remember walking onto the stage at my high school graduation and fighting back the tears as I made my way halfway across. I could not shake the overwhelming feeling of accomplishment; my emotions were going wild, yet it felt good! I was the first person in my mum's family to graduate! I did it! I did that! Truth be told, the more I achieved over the years, the more I wanted. I wanted to be successful, and I was just getting started. That night, the confidence to believe in myself and to know that I could achieve everything my heart desired was fueled, and more so with every other graduation or accomplishment that followed.

Embracing Your Why

Before you can truly commit to the personal qualities, habits, and attributes that support professional success, you must first understand and embrace your "WHY." Why do you want to achieve this? Will your dream keep driving you? Will it make you jump out of bed every morning, especially on the days that you do not feel like it? Where will this dream, or desire, take you in five years, or even ten years? Understanding your "why" will give you the purpose and passion needed to pursue your dreams. I will keep it real with you; experience has taught me that some people are hungry to learn and grow, while others are quite contented where they are. Being able to pay the bills will simply be enough for some, but for persons that are driven or hungry to achieve the personal goals and aspirations they have set for their lives, a strong purpose is likely to be an underlying factor. Before you can focus on pursuing your life goals, you will absolutely need to understand your "purpose" and "where we want to be"; you must have a vision for your life. Understanding these aspects of yourself will help you shape the habits and attitude that you will embrace throughout your life. The personal attributes of perseverance, commitment, excellence, gratitude, and consistency all start to take shape once you have identified and truly connected with a deeper purpose.

The underlying reasons that drive my career performance today pretty much remain the same as when I was getting started. Knowing that my efforts and contribution are valued and highly regarded now acts as an example to others, including my daughter. Part of my "why" is still very much centered around maintaining high levels of excellence in everything I do, while putting myself in a position to help others, whether it be watching them grow professionally or, in my family's case, being able to offer some level of financial support, when warranted.

Leveraging Your Purpose for Success

In pursuit of your career journey, there will be so many times when you will need to draw on your purpose. T. D. Jakes always says, "if you can't figure out your purpose, figure out your passion for your passion will lead you right into your purpose." The ability to reflect and relate to your purpose is what will get you over many obstacles, and trust me, the obstacles will come. According to the team at Leadership First, "if you manage a team, your why is what will keep you inspired to keep pushing, help you to share positive stories to inspire others, help you to stay on track even when the journey appears off track and keep you getting out of bed every morning when the challenges arise."

Personally, my favorite buzz line is, *"you have to love what you do!"* However, loving what you do is heavily dependent on your understanding of why you are doing what you are doing. Does the immediate action, or collective actions, really make you happy or provide some sort of instant gratification? Or is it the long-term outcome that is driving you? Sometimes, the realization that where you are is where you are supposed to be in your journey will be enough to see you through. At other times, depending on the intensity of the challenge, only a deep-rooted passion can provide that much-needed thrust that motivates you to push past every obstacle.

There is value in stepping back from a situation in order to step forward, but many times, the path forward may require a shift in mindset. As you peruse the following pages of this book, I challenge you to commit some quiet time to better understand your purpose. Make a conscious effort to understand what it is that truly drives you and, believe me, your future self will thank you for it.

Attitude Is Everything

"A positive attitude is like a new Superpower!"

$\mathcal{S}$ome people appear misled by the myth that there is a secret recipe to success. Let me assure you, this is totally not the case. There are, however, some common themes that are evident amongst the most successful leaders and business owners. Personal qualities such as passion, positive mindset, discipline, and consistency are embedded into their daily lives. From my own experience, these may prove to be the most important skills of all time. Persons that possess this unique combination are almost always likely to make a greater impact.

Through observation and mentorship of others, my general view is that too many people fail to build consistency and show genuine passion; I may even go so far as to say that this may result from fundamental flaws in their overall attitude. Simply put, many employees need to get their attitudes in check! Yes, it needed to be said, especially for employees with strong technical capabilities and know-how who continue to get overlooked for career advancement opportunities or fail to positively influence their peers or other decision makers. Almost a hundred percent of times, this happens when something about the employee's attitude is what I generally refer to as "off." To quote my favorite author, John C. Maxwell, "The greatest day in our lives is when we take total responsibility for our attitudes. That's the day we truly grow up!" One of the most valuable lessons I learned early in my career is that attitude matters. How many employees today are truly willing to take the important step of evaluating their own attitude? Way too often, the natural response is to look outward for others to blame or for all sorts of other excuses versus pausing for a moment to be introspective, ultimately examining the attitude they bring to the job and in particular, their interaction with others. Rightfully or wrongfully, "perception is reality," and having a positive attitude often helps to manage "intent versus outcome" in your actions.

This hit me like a ton of bricks when I first entered the banking industry at eighteen years old to work on a short-term project. I was quickly identified as the project lead and later selected from among five other young professionals for an extended contract. As inexperienced as I was at the time, it was quite evident that the only difference between the other team members and myself was the overall attitude I brought to the job. It was not like I was any smarter; as a matter of fact, my peers were all fresh University graduates while I had only just completed a Business Studies certificate. The real fact was that, as tedious as the project was, I maintained an overall positive outlook and worked feverishly to keep the project on track, while others slacked off because they had become bored and lost interest in the project. My decision to remain assertive and accept accountability for the entire project, including pulling the extra weight, surely did not go unnoticed. Furthermore, I intentionally sought out other unrelated tasks to help break the monotony of the project (as truth be told, the project really was boring as heck). This approach resulted in me forging some really cool relationships with other employees who sought to mentor me and, without even realizing it, I had repositioned myself into an "unofficial" role within the company, ultimately strengthening my value and contribution.

As a business leader, I find it truly admirable that our young professionals today are quite ambitious. Unfortunately, too many fail to realize that failure to go beyond the normal expectations of the role will cause them to never stand out amongst their peers. My daughter absolutely hates when I use the word "average," but the point must be made that way too many average employees do exist; adopting the minimalist approach and somehow expecting to see maximum returns. Don't get me wrong, all employees can make a contribution; however, it must be clearly understood that this approach does not lend to sustainable growth and career advancement. The simple reality is that you have to be prepared to put in the extra work, and this will only be sustainable if you have made a conscious decision to evaluate and adjust your attitude.

Get Your Attitude Right!

With each passing day, you have a choice as a career professional:

- To be proactive or reactive.
- To strive consistently for excellence and not only when others are watching.
- To be passionate about success and bring the right energy to the job versus doing just enough to get by.
- To take genuine pride in how you consistently present yourself in order to build executive presence.
- To be solutions-oriented or be labeled as a complainer.
- To make decisions and take actions that align to the company's vision and your own personal goals.

- To be an avid team player or seek individual recognition.
- To be approachable or deter other team members with your irrational reactions.
- Will you adopt what I describe as the victim-mentality or seek to first understand?
- Will you forget about the title for the moment and choose to lead, or will you follow?
- Will you focus on the positives or pick at every flaw and risk earning the label of being negative?
- Will you respect your peers and their views, or will you avoid any real collaboration?
- Will you share your knowledge and remain teachable or be intimidated by the growth of others?
- Will you truly accept constructive feedback and take action or throw your hands in the air and feel sorry for yourself?

Of course, I can go on, but the thing to note is that we have a choice every single day regarding the attitude we embrace. We choose how we respond to circumstances. We must decide where we want to go and what matters the most. How we go about achieving both our personal and professional goals will be very much wrapped up in our overall attitude and the perception of others. Maintaining a positive attitude supported by the right level of passion and energy will breed endurance and consistency, which will surely produce a win for your career and life in general.

It is absolutely important to examine your current attitude and, where necessary, seek feedback from others (preferably not your closest allies, unless they are brutally honest). You simply cannot do the same and stay the same and expect any real change. Dedicate a quiet moment to assess your current situation and solicit feedback if you need to but be sure to accept the feedback as it comes and commit to a new game plan. Take accountability for your actions and execute that new plan with such rigor that those around you may not be able to understand. Do bear in mind that during this shift, some close friends or associates may pull away and, trust me, that is okay. These people may not fit within the future God has planned for your life anyway.

As a business leader, I no longer hire for technical ability over attitude and fit. Both are now of equal importance, and if I must choose, rest assured, attitude will win each and every time. You must understand that your current attitude can determine your altitude. And always remember that your attitude is like a price tag. It shows others how valuable you are. Your attitude makes a big difference to your final outcome, so be conscious of the fact that people hear your words but feel your attitude and, ultimately, that's the real deciding factor that can positively or negatively affect your future.

Get Up, Get Dressed, and Show Up!

"You don't have to be extreme! Just be consistent."

The life of a career professional comes with its fair share of challenges. To stay ahead of the game, I maintain a positive outlook and try to live by one simple rule, regardless of how I am feeling or what is going on in my fast-paced life. I *"Get Up, Get Dressed, and Show Up."* That's right. And on days that I am faced with my greatest challenges or even feeling at my lowest, I make a conscious effort to get even more dressed up! This personal mantra has been responsible for many of my accomplishments over the years. This behavior and mindset breeds consistency and goes a long way toward shaping the perception of others and, by extension, your personal brand. Without consistency in your approach, it is really hard to positively influence others or lead to any real significant change in your life.

Some days, masked behind the fancy corporate suit, flawless make up, and a beaming smile, I am struggling to make it through the day for one reason or the other. Guess what, very few people can tell. Over the years, many persons have asked me how I do it. First of all, let me say upfront that I am not a fake, nor is this preferred disposition a pretense. I learned early in my career that in order to make any real progress in this life, you have to show up, and you have to do so consistently. This means being prepared at all times for whatever comes your way; the planned, the impromptu, and the unexpected. Whether it be a business meeting or pursuing personal endeavors, it will be difficult to have any real impact unless you show up ready to apply yourself and take on the challenges.

From observation, there are many people who want change, yet are unwilling to take the simplest step of just showing up prepared. How else do you claim what is yours or make the steps necessary to achieve your goals if you do not show up? After watching my mother go to work on the plantation after losing her job at the factory come rain, sunshine, and even illness, I somehow managed to convince myself that if I didn't always show up, someone would claim what was rightfully mine. This mindset really forces you to push yourself, day in and day out, particularly on the days when you feel like you have already reached your limit. The ultimate test is sustaining this approach when you are not operating at your physical best. Ironically, and at times to my own detriment without even realizing it, I have mastered the art of masking the pain, followed by a lightning bolt crash at the end of my workday, which remains unexplainable up to this day. Truth be told, I can only rationalize the level of grit and stamina I have acquired over the years as a special gift from God.

Unless you are born into money or, as the older folk say, "with a gold spoon in your mouth," success only comes when you get up and go. It is always great to dream of a better life, but unless those dreams turn into goals with specific action plans, along with a few genuine supporters in your corner, you are very likely to go off track. When I look back at my life, I don't think many people expected me to reach this level. I was never considered a bright spark, yet I knew I was steady, so I refused to focus my attention on the naysayers. As I moved through my twenties, I became laser focused on the goals I had set for my life. Thankfully, I always had my mum in my corner to snap me back into reality when I thought it was okay to wander off or entertain distractions at times. Bringing your best game every day calls for a high degree of commitment, and I do not necessarily mean commitment to the job, school, or other pursuits; more so, commitment to "self-improvement." When you reach the stage in your life where you are certain of what you want to accomplish, "commitment" and "consistency" must become your default disposition. You must remain purpose-driven! Overtime, the habit of "getting up, getting dressed, and showing up" will prove worthwhile in shaping the important personal qualities that are needed to build a strong foundation and jumpstart your journey. Without a doubt, however, this should be supported by a flexible career game plan.

Consider Your Game Plan

"If you are serious about where you want to be and what you visualize for your life, don't leave your career progress to chance."

I once came across this quote that read, "A satisfied life is better than a successful life as our success tends to be measured by others, while our satisfaction is measured by our heart, mind, and soul." This really set me thinking about the importance of pursuing a career journey that brings personal satisfaction. I was also reminded that it is vitally important that we recognize that people define success differently, and that is perfectly acceptable. What is even more evident is that personal satisfaction is more likely when you plan for success based on our own dreams and aspirations.

Years ago, I remember performing a junior manager role that I was really good at but truth be told, gave me very little satisfaction. The job literally felt like a chore and what was worst was I felt trapped because everyone saw me as the subject matter expert. The sheer thought of spending another year in the role was at times suffocating. The reality, however, is that when you fail to create a career game plan, you can default to performing roles based on your knowledge, experience, and skill set. As part of your career planning process, you need to give some real thought to where you want to be within the next five to ten years. Furthermore, you need to consider the path required to get there. As a person who has never held a single role for more than three years during the early stages of my career, I can assure you that each role change was strategically aligned with my long-term career plan.

Many professionals today have no idea what they genuinely want to accomplish or where they are headed, let alone taking the time to design a clear plan that defines how you will achieve those goals. You must have a game plan! I was really hopeful that the newly embraced concept of creating vision boards would have moved beyond encapsulating the theme "don't wait for it, create it". More so by examining practical approaches that support the actual execution process.

In 2010, after wrapping up what would have been my last Senior Leaders Regional Conference at the Bank, one of my direct leaders enquired why I was not joining the team for dinner later that evening. I explained that the time I had spent planning the event and preparing multiple conference presentations had unfortunately caused me to be lagging behind in an MBA assignment that was due for submission. The Director, for whom I have plenty of respect and with whom I enjoyed working proceeded to ask me, "why are you even bothering to pursue the program at the time, considering your current work demands? You have such a bright future ahead in the bank," he added.

Mind you, I did not doubt for one second that I had a bright future ahead, but I refused to take any comfort in this endorsement or vote of confidence. I was certain that my immediate plan included garnering all the practical strategic leadership experience

I could, balanced with pursuing my professional qualifications. Ultimately, after joining the bank at such a young age and spending over thirteen years in the same organization, I had this underlying desire to explore whether I had acquired transferable skills that would allow me to also succeed in another organization or even in a completely different industry. Based on my career game plan, I knew the time would come when I would eventually move on from the bank. Notwithstanding, this never once negatively influenced my commitment or performance; more so, it pushed me harder to create a strong personal brand where over time, I became known for maintaining exceptionally high performance standards.

Ironically, despite my passion for continuous improvement, I am not one for focusing on long-term professional goals. As a mentor, my preference is always to help others identify short to medium term SMART goals (specific, measurable, attainable, relevant, and time-bound), since the rate of growth in business today requires ongoing agility and flexibility. You should always be prepared to quickly pivot or adjust your course of action without losing sight of your long-term game plan.

Having a game plan for your future helps you avoid being boxed into the vision others have for your life. It also helps to better evaluate the opportunities presented to ensure that these are aligned to your desired goals. The practice of reassessing your game plan from time to time with the support of a trusted mentor adds considerable value and can help you to refocus and, at times, even identify when it is necessary to get back on track. Success is by no means an accident and will require you to be intentional, which over time will help you to create the discipline needed in your approach.

It is equally important to understand that execution of your life's plan will come with some degree of personal sacrifice. If an opportunity aligns with your personal goals, you must be prepared to make those sacrifices. Being mindful that in pursuit of your dreams, you may also be labeled differently from your peers; it would prove useful to accept this early on in your career and keep pressing forward. I once read somewhere that "when we have a plan and a burning desire to bring our plan to life, the desire to succeed should be as strong as our desire to breathe" because only then do we truly shape the most important qualities needed for success.

There is no better time than now to give some thought to whether you are presently on the right path for the vision you have set for your life. Or is it that you now need to define your vision? Either way, it is okay, because every new day brings about a new opportunity to reassess your situation. From my own experience, it really does not matter where you are in the journey once you become truly committed to where you are heading. One thing is certain: if you want to be in control of your own destiny, you must possess a game plan and go about your journey being deliberate in all that you do.

"There is so much more to Personal Branding but believe me when I tell you that the way you present yourself matters."

Personal Branding
Is Real

> "Visualize your highest self and show up as that person every day!"
>
> —Unknown

*W*hether you know it or not, you have a personal brand that speaks to the reputation and legacy you are creating, within both your personal and professional life. Many people link personal branding to how you look and what styles you wear, yet personal branding goes way beyond this. Your personal brand is tied to the core values you exhibit, the personal vision you have for yourself, and the outward image you ultimately portray to others based on your performance. Your personal brand should come alive as part of the process of connecting with others and, based on my own experience, the best personal brands are persons that remain true to who they are and still manage to capture the hearts of others, while inspiring others they don't even realize are watching. A strong personal brand can lead to career opportunities; in contrast, a weak personal brand presents the risk of being overlooked. Several factors can affect your personal brand. Throughout my life, I was intent on avoiding the labels generally affixed to those coming from lower socio-economic backgrounds while working to carve out my own personal brand as I set off to create the vision I had for my life.

The Importance of Personal Branding

Have you ever wondered what is the first thing that comes to mind when someone that can influence your future thinks of you? More so, have you ever done a Google search of yourself to see what pops up? With both scenarios, you can almost immediately see the need to be intentional in shaping your personal brand. In this era of social media, the focus on personal branding has become even more essential. We always hear the phrase, "you never get a second chance to make a first impression." Personally, I always interpreted this to mean that the first impression should be one that will set you apart from others, builds trust, and provides a true reflection of who you are. In my early days managing a frontline team and as part of the thrust toward service excellence, I always created a picture for the team to understand that their future boss could be sitting right in front of them one day. This was not just as a means of fostering an exceptional service culture, but more so to highlight the need to always maintain consistently high standards in support of their own personal brand. Furthermore, during the first couple years of working with my current boss, I treated every meeting like an interview. I was always over-prepared! This was not at all because I was uncomfortable in any aspect of our working relationship; I was quite conscious that I was in a new organization and that my personal brand was still very much a work in progress.

Creating Your Personal Brand Identity

First off, to create your personal brand, you need to understand your "why." What really drives you, and what are you passionate about? Where are you headed, and what do you want to be known for? Without this clear picture in mind, it becomes much harder to build and develop consistency in bringing your personal brand to life. As a transformational leader, I live and breathe continuous improvement, and not just for the products and services we offer to the market. The ability to influence my team's development, both individually and collectively, is a personal win that gives me the greatest satisfaction. Of equal importance, however, is my own self-development, which remains high on my agenda. John C. Maxwell suggests that "true leaders never stop learning." For me, this means staying on top of developments in my chosen field, reading articles on topics that I am passionate about, and seeking to expand my knowledge on areas where I can add real value to others. If you are to truly create a strong personal brand, you must stay committed to learning and sharing with others as you seek to remain relevant and to make an impactful contribution.

Building Your Personal Brand

I am by no means an expert, but I can assure you that consistency is extremely important in building your personal branding. The marketing concept of "on-brand" and "off-brand" also applies to personal branding. In creating and living your personal brand inspired by your core values and personal vision, it took me sometime to realize that *you have to keep your energy right and your circle tight.* Never allow your personal brand to be derailed by others. Oprah Winfrey reminds us to "always surround yourself with people who are going to lift you higher." Having self-confidence and self-belief is important when seeking to build a strong personal brand, but you must never lose yourself in the process. Understand and embrace your roots and passion!

"Perception is reality" becomes even more relevant in personal branding, so ensure your daily actions are intentional and filled with passion. Be mindful, however, that without integrity, your personal brand can be ruined before it even gets started. Persons must be able to trust you, and you must live up to who you say you are. Inconsistencies in your personal qualities and character only make it difficult to connect with, influence, or inspire others. *Always remain genuine and true to who you are.* This approach will ensure that your character does not appear unreliable when presented with certain situations.

If you are truly serious about building your personal brand, a good approach is to become a subject matter expert. Becoming the "go-to" requires you to be so competent in your chosen field so that you remain at the top of everyone's mind.

Last, but by no means least, believe it when I tell you that *the way you present yourself matters*! Your personal style goes back to the image you wish to portray, so you absolutely need to always be on-brand. Sorry, but you do not get to have off days (unless you are sick in bed of course). Despite being financially strapped early in my career, I quickly learned the importance of always looking the part. I remember investing in plain black skirts and career pants with a few nice tops. Today, as I interact with other professionals across my network, so many people ask me, "how do you manage to always look so put together?" Guess what, it is part of my personal brand! So, regardless of how I am feeling or what is going on in my life, I get up, I get dressed, and I show up!

For us ladies, building a personal brand is a little more complex. As a woman leader, I suggest that you lose the really tight or short pieces for work as the look sometimes suggests you are trying too hard. Not to mention that we work in a world dominated by males and should always seek to be taken seriously on the merit of our work. If you are budget conscious, try to mix and match and try new colors and styles. For the office, light make up, a presentable hairstyle, and complementary bag and shoes completes your overall look. Get in the habit of asking yourself each day before heading out the door, "will my presence in the room add, subtract, or complement?" Recognizing that new office cultures are constantly evolving. Over the years, I have adopted the practice of getting even more dressed up on the days that I am feeling at my lowest as this really helps to lift my mood and energy for the day ahead.

Personal branding is real, so pause for a moment and give some thought to where you are, where you want to be, and whether your current brand will take you there. A combination of self-evaluation, striving to deliver high performance standards while building consistency, coupled with a personable appearance and positive attitude will definitely see your personal brand starting to come alive before you even realize it.

The Growth Factor

*"If someone offers you an amazing opportunity
and you're not sure you can do it, say yes—and
then figure out how to do it later!"*

—Richard Branson

Have you ever wondered why you or someone you know that is great at their job keeps getting overlooked for career opportunities? Typically, employees who possess a growth mindset exhibit certain qualities that cause them to stand out amongst their peers. They tend to be passionate about learning, finding solutions, and making a difference, all encapsulated in a positive attitude. Leaders are definitely more likely to have the confidence that this type of employee will get the job done, which in turn fuels the overall growth and development of the employee, even in cases where they may have lacked certain technical ability. The quote by Richard Branson holds true as a career winning strategy. During my tenure in banking, it took me a while to realize that I was being earmarked for roles long before I even made the decision to apply. This was mostly because of my growing personal brand reputation, proactive nature, and ongoing willingness to learn and grow.

Passion Over Talent Any Day

Employees with a growth mindset are passionate about identifying and executing continuous improvement opportunities, while bringing an overall positive approach to their daily routine. These employees often accept accountability for tasks outside of their core responsibilities and see any failures as new learning opportunities. Ironically, many times, this type of employee might not be the most talented in the team nor even the subject matter expert. Way too many employees today possess an entitlement mentality and somehow prefer to focus their energy on complaining and making excuses instead of proactively seeking solutions. This mindset causes the employee to lose sight of the bigger picture; failing to see new challenges, obstacles, or any extended contribution on their part as an opportunity to learn, grow, and cultivate greater capacity.

After one year of literally bouncing around from role to role within the prestigious Barclays Mortgage Unit very early in my career, I successfully landed myself a full-time job. My stint was totally rewarding, despite the year-long uncertainty around my employment status. After the six-week project, I was hired to work on came to a close, I assumed the self-proclaimed and unofficial role of "Relief Officer" within the business unit. My work days, which I am certain many would have found extremely frustrating, saw me bouncing around from desk to desk assisting other team members and proactively filling any voids within the unit in order to sustain efficiency; not to mention taking on any special projects that the full-time team had no time nor interest in pursuing.

While the demands on my time grew rapidly, so did my knowledge, skills, and experience. I was eager to learn, so I remained teachable, and not once did I allow any negativity to step in, nor did I feed off the vibe of other team members who frequently thought I was being exploited. At eighteen years old without any major academic qualifications, I was learning about mortgage collateral requirements and the associated insurance, bank reconciliations, insurance products, delivering first class service, and so much more. *I was on an intentional path to jumpstart my career, quickly realizing that an open mindset and a positive attitude, filled with gratitude for all opportunities provided were important ingredients in my journey to success.*

Don't Wait for It. Create It!

People with a growth mindset feel empowered and are eager to share their suggestions and ideas with leaders and peers while welcoming the opportunity to receive feedback. They tend to leverage their strengths to bring about continuous improvements while recognizing areas of weakness. They exhibit the confidence to engage with others and are always focused on ensuring the best solutions are presented or implemented. Persons who are truly focused on growth rarely focus on the obstacles, only on the opportunities, and are willing to go the extra mile or two while remaining accountable for the task at hand. *Simply put, they give it their all, because they are passionate about what they do and are keen to make a real difference.*

As part of your growth strategy, you should be sure to seek constant feedback. You should never underestimate the power of feedback, yet you must be truly ready to receive it and take action. Feedback on your overall performance or how you handle certain situations can come from your direct manager, supervisors, a mentor or coach, and even your peers. Only persons that can objectively offer you constructive feedback should ever be engaged as a part of your growth plan. Trust me, we all need those persons in our life who care enough to tell us the cold, hard truth when required! As a general rule, feedback from close friends should only be solicited if they possess the ability to remain unbiased with a clear appreciation for helping you achieve your future goals. Be forewarned, though, that not all feedback received will sit well with you and that is okay. Once you get over the initial shock or hurt, be ready to take intentional action. Equally, not everyone who offers you feedback will have your best interest at heart. They say, if it does not challenge you, it doesn't change you! My advice is to always remain flexible and adaptable to change. A growth mindset requires that you remain willing to try new things and new approaches.

One year, in a 360-leadership review, the CEO scored me as average under the category of "taking risks." Next to all the above average scores, this stuck out like a sore thumb on the assessment report. He went even further commenting on his reason for the score, highlighting that my preference was to always make calculated decisions. This feedback sent me in an instant state of reflection, because I knew he was absolutely correct. Nevertheless, I knew at that very moment that I would need to find a way to address this deep-rooted thought process. I quickly started examining specific cases that I could have been handled differently. This process was crucial if I were to improve my overall performance and ultimately the perception of others going forward. Many employees go into performance reviews ready to dispute what they perceived to be unfavorable scores. The real value comes from treating the highlighted areas raised during the performance management process as an opportunity for growth. That being said, the approach adopted by some managers is not at all conducive for fueling professional growth. As a leader, your approach should be to provide frequent and ongoing feedback to team members so that the performance review process brings little to no surprises.

Growth Challenge

If you are truly ready to grow and excel in your current field, start using opportunities that you are granted or that fall within your reach as a platform for professional growth. Your willingness to participate and even lead some projects will go a long way in shaping your career growth plan and personal brand. Be mindful that if your first thought after contributing outside of your established role is linked to the need for an increase in salary or recognition, your mindset is really not completely repositioned for growth.

For clarity, I am by no means advocating for you to be exploited; simply that you realize that extraordinary work seldom goes unnoticed and is generally followed by amazing returns. Focusing on increasing your performance and creating value by raising your hand to volunteer for tasks is an excellent growth strategy. However, the real value comes from doing this without expecting any applause, recognition, or rewards. You must never allow the desire to be recognized or rewarded become more important than your ultimate performance. A great practice to adopt would be to make your contribution bigger than your reward. Simply put, adopting a zero-entitlement attitude and performing in such a way that causes a positive impact will most definitely cause you to get noticed, further fueling your growth.

Ultimately, the success that you have been waiting for sits outside your comfort zone, yet squarely within your control. Allow your desire to grow and your passion to succeed drive your contribution and, rest assured, the best is yet to follow.

Growth and Gratitude

"If you are doing what you do for reward and recognition, you are already off to a wrong start!"

In the previous chapter, I spoke in-depth to the importance of possessing a growth mindset and the type of attributes required to truly position yourself for professional growth. Passion over talent continues to be emphasized as a core ingredient for success as it provides the courage and tenacity necessary to overcome the challenges faced throughout the professional journey. Employees who are passionate about what they do tend to focus heavily on continuous improvement of self and the impact they can make within the business and take pride in their overall contribution. Consistency continues to be highlighted as an extremely important attribute for anyone with a growth mindset. Yet, there is another important aspect that we must consider on the journey to success. *Gratitude Shifts Your Mindset!* As the saying goes *"gratitude changes everything and what you appreciate, appreciates."*

As you embark on your career, reposition yourself within your organization, or start up a new business, cultivating an attitude of gratitude can have a significant impact on your overall progress.

This approach highlights to your supervisors, managers, team leads, or other key influencers that you are truly appreciative of the opportunities afforded to you, causing you to remain top of mind for future opportunities and projects.

Gratitude Brings Rewards

During my first year as Marketing Officer, supporting a team of newly hired managers tasked with building out the bank's suite of credit card products across the Caribbean region, I was literally drowning in work. Also new to my role, I found myself being pulled left to right by the five managers who had really aggressive strategic plans and growth targets. Furthermore, our leader depended heavily on me to coordinate, track, and report on the unit's progress, in addition to my other core supporting tasks. Being the "go-to" for a team of high-performance, high-demanding managers who were laser focused and moving faster than lightning, presented a real challenge that forced me to quickly up my game (*sometimes, I think I worked harder that year than any other year throughout my entire career*).

By the end of the first year, I had successfully built new relationships and put processes and other structures in place to ensure that I was "working smarter and not harder." Of course, staying ahead of the team was necessary to effectively manage the unit, which saw me making a number of personal sacrifices. Ultimately, the feedback received on my performance that first year was all the motivation I needed to keep going! By the beginning of the following year, the management team was approved to visit the London-based Barclaycard Center. And guess what, I too was selected to join the team. Needless to say, I could not contain my excitement knowing that I was going on my first business trip even though I did not even own a passport at the time. The travel experience was unimaginable, and the knowledge acquired during the week-long training took me, my performance, and my contribution within the unit to a whole new level.

The practice of going above and beyond and setting my standards higher than anyone expected of me is what really afforded me that amazing development opportunity. At this point, the importance of doing the right thing consistently, remaining grateful for each opportunity presented to learn and grow, and allowing the rewards to follow became crystal clear. As John C. Maxwell suggests, the best version of you is a grateful you.

Gratitude Is a Must

While positioning yourself for growth, you will find yourself functioning outside of your comfort zone, as the two simply do not coexist; whether this comes in the form of having to acquire new skills to complete a task or embracing constructive feedback from your leaders or peers. Having an attitude of gratitude throughout your career journey causes you to express thankfulness for the opportunities presented in both your professional and personal life. It also helps you to balance any negativity that may creep in when challenges arise, allowing you to see setbacks simply as teaching moments.

Embracing gratitude as a recipe for success also helps to foster better relationships within the workplace while helping to influence your inner circle and network in support of building a strong personal brand. Showing genuine appreciation for colleagues, mentors, and key influencers that guide you along your professional journey should remain top of mind. To this day, I make a special effort to stay connected to all my past leaders or close colleagues who were instrumental to my career development. Bear in mind, adopting a negative attitude or ungrateful disposition can derail or block your blessings. It is important to realize that new opportunities will continue to be presented to those employees most grateful for their past experiences.

Starting today, ensure that expressions of gratitude remain prevalent as you embark on what will be a more rewarding journey. This transition will allow you to shift your focus to creating more value, as you continue raising the bar. To quote Oprah Winfrey, *"you should practice being thankful for what you have; you will end up having more. If you concentrate on what you don't have, you will never, ever have enough!"*

The Power of Discipline

"God if you pull it, I swear I will push it! Day in and day out, I will bring my best game."

—Sarah Jake-Roberts

To be honest, life has a way of getting overly busy at times, causing us to go off track or delay our pursuit of other important goals and dreams. I have come to realize that the secret to our future success lies in our daily routine. Applying a considerable degree of discipline as a part of your development game plan is key to sustaining both personal and professional progress. Discipline helps build the level of consistency necessary to not only achieve but sustain success. I do not recall where I read this statement, "There are two types of people in this world, the persons who wait until they feel like it before they do it, and the persons who say they have to do it so they feel like it." Ask yourself, which one are you?

Let me say upfront, if you do not have discipline, you can forget the prize, because winners possess a high degree of discipline. You cannot always be motivated (never) so you must learn to be disciplined. Discipline is what keeps you going on the days you just do not feel like moving out of bed. Furthermore, it provides the willpower to push to complete a task or project that no longer motivates you but still needs to get done. The ability to perform above average, meet deadlines, and keep your life on schedule are all key benefits of self-discipline. You must adopt a disciplined approach toward accomplishing your goals, especially in today's competitive work environment where leaders are looking to retain their best talent. Mind you, even those fortunate enough to be born into wealth display a high degree of discipline, because they understand the importance of securing their assets in order to generate greater wealth for future generations.

Being disciplined is not always easy and sometimes literally requires a paradigm shift in how we train our mind, thoughts, and actions. Always acknowledging that "anything worth doing, simply needs to get done" has been at the core of my performance over the years. Many persons ask me, "How do you do it? When do you find the time to get it all done?" First off, I try to invest my time in activities that I am truly passionate about, and secondly, once I commit to something, I tend to give it my all. Don't be fooled, many times, because of my busy schedule tied to the demands of my job and my roles with other associations and other personal projects, this calls for endurance and a heavy reliance on discipline to take me across the finish line. Focusing on the end state or desired outcome generally helps sustain commitment throughout the journey.

The real test came when I was completing my MBA program. Balancing a highly demanding job where I supported over twenty regional Senior Executives, while raising my two-year-old and dealing with crippling migraine headaches; trust me, I was just about to give up. My life was full to capacity, causing me to constantly ask myself "What the heck am I doing? Will this really be worth it in the end? How will I ever get this done?" During this highly stressful time, I literally had to force myself to develop a new level of discipline in order to push forward. At the end of this intense phase, I had a greater appreciation for the power of endurance—realizing that what doesn't break you makes you stronger—in addition to realizing how important it is to focus on the purpose behind why you are doing what you are doing, in order to finish what you started.

Discipline as a New Superpower

The ability to control your *thoughts* and *actions* is probably one of the greatest superpowers you will ever possess. The world's greatest leaders all speak about how essential discipline is in order to unlock your fullest potential. The ability to push past procrastination, low motivation levels, and even frustration at times, are solely tied to your mindset and level of discipline.

In *21 Irrefutable Laws of Leadership*, John C. Maxwell suggests that "momentum is a leader's best friend." Based on my own experience, I can absolutely assure you that you will fail to build any real momentum without discipline and consistency. Balancing life in general can be very challenging. The practice of knocking off routine tasks early in your work week or day can prove amazingly effective and even create some quick wins that help you build that much-needed momentum. As an added benefit, this level of consistency allows time for creative thinking and strategic planning of other important initiatives. The simple truth is that people who possess the power of discipline are better equipped to accomplish so much more than others.

Now is the time to embrace that "must-do, can-do, will-do" attitude, supported by greater levels of self-discipline. You will be amazed at how much more you can get done. Remembering always that you are the single biggest influence over your life.

Embracing Accountability

"Growth is a silent investment! It doesn't speak up,
it shows up!"

—Unknown

In the early years of my career, I found myself constantly taking on special projects and other tasks that were indirectly linked to my specific role. Truthfully, while many colleagues continued to argue that I was being exploited by management, I was intentionally and purposefully building the foundation necessary to set my career on the right path. The willingness to take responsibility for special projects quickly saw me interacting more with Supervisors and Managers. My opinion started to matter and, at times, I was the only junior employee at the planning or decision-making table.

As a leader, more and more I am noticing that "soft skills" such as taking accountability, exhibiting passion, and consistent use of initiative are traits not widely being practiced by many of today's young professionals. In discussions with other business leaders, there is almost unanimous agreement that too many employees wish to advance their careers but refuse to build the foundation necessary by "actually putting in the work," in some cases, even failing to take accountability for their own professional development. As a consequence, it is now remarkably easy for leaders to spot exceptional team members who are striving to make a difference and are prepared to stand up and accept responsibility. This situation calls for further consideration as we examine why many employees are so unwilling to accept accountability, even at times when it falls squarely within their deliverables. Could this approach be due to fear of failure, lack of employee engagement, or downright laziness? As an eternal optimist, I pray this mindset is not driven by fear of failure since this tends to have a more crippling effect on self-development.

Believe it or not, fear and failure can both be used to our advantage, ultimately leading to positive career advancement. It has been proven time and time again that employees who are not afraid to accept responsibility will actively learn and quickly develop important leadership skills. The real benefit of stepping forward is in highlighting your ability to juggle multiple deliverables, which helps expand your scope and capacity and, more importantly, positions you as a dependable self-starter.

Does this approach require some level of sacrifice? Of course, it does! Will you always reap immediate rewards or recognition? Most definitely not. Employees who are not captivated by fear and are willing to make an intentional effort to step outside of their comfort zone to take on more responsibility are generally more exposed to a range of strategic planning and decision-making techniques. This helps raise capacity levels through new learnings, which collectively results in company-wide exposure and repositioning of your overall value and contribution. The reality is that new opportunities will continue to be presented in the work environment, and leaders are always looking to spot their best talent.

So, what advice would I share with young professionals seeking to advance their careers or to excel in their current roles? There really is no secret recipe. However, if you are focused on your personal and professional growth, you must be willing to step forward. Stop hiding behind defined roles or fear of failure. In order to stand out amongst your peers and be taken seriously, you must start to view new tasks, projects, or assignments as a real opportunity to enhance both technical and soft skills, which will help to shape your career advancement opportunities.

In today's rapidly changing business environment, this approach will also provide an opportunity to develop five core skills (5 Cs) that will prove necessary for achieving success:

1. Increased **Capacity**
2. Effective **Communication**
3. Ability to make new **Connections**
4. **Critical Thinking** and
5. **Consistency**

I appreciate that this approach may cause some to ponder. Rest assured that if you are truly serious about your professional progress, it is absolutely important to build a core foundation. Be intentional about stepping outside of your comfort zone in order to acquire these important competencies that will better position you to not only get ahead but to stay ahead.

Managing Risks

"If we are growing, we are always going to be outside our comfort zone."

—John C. Maxwell

During my early days at the managerial level, I would have to admit that I was never really good at making quick decisions that involved any degree of risks. I had a clear preference for making factual and practical decisions where I could predict a high probability of success. While this may sound like a positive attribute, I started to learn that leadership requires you to be much more prepared to take calculated risks at a faster rate. Today's leaders must be prepared to "fail fast" and "fail forward" in order to build greater capacity and to be effective in this highly complex world.

In working to develop this skill, I often wondered where this need to always have everything under control came from. It seemed to be a deep-rooted trait that may have been influenced by my early childhood. Living with so much uncertainty day in and day out clearly had an impact on my desire for structure in my way of life. Whether it be my work schedule and projects, managing my finances, my relationships, and even my living space, I always performed much better when there was a clear plan and approach. Whatever the root cause, it served me well during my early years but was certainly not going to prove a successful strategy as I entered a new phase of leadership that required a slightly different approach.

The biggest challenge was reshaping my approach to decision-making in the face of my rapidly evolving professional responsibilities and executive demands. You see, senior leadership requires decisive action in the face of ongoing uncertainty due to ever changing regulations, more demanding and digitally savvy customers, evolving employee rights, along with the need for the business to be more innovative in order to secure market competitiveness. I was forced to push past my aversion to risk if I was going to be successful.

Thankfully, over time, experience taught me critical thinking techniques for balancing the level of risk and exposure when making important business decisions. I came to the realization that in order for me to continue growing and be successful at the next level of leadership, I would need to first adopt a more intentional approach to the way I managed and evaluated business scenarios. This saw me focusing more on the "what if" scenarios. My new way of thinking became, "if the original plan does not work, then what? Can we afford to take the chance? How will this decision impact our customers, and if so, how many? How will it impact the team?"

My approach to being team-centric, customer-centric, and solution-centric started to reshape my approach to leadership and augured well for fostering a solutions-focused company culture. Thankfully, today, I am very pragmatic with the ability to assess situations quickly and offer viable options and solutions, but this did not come easy for me. As I prepared this manuscript, I started to reflect on the events in my past that could have influenced my initial aversion to managing risks.

At nine years old, after my mum lost her job at the computer parts firm due to redundancy, she began working on a nearby plantation in order to put food on the table. The transition made an already tough situation even worse for my family, though I secretly enjoyed the extra time we were now able to spend together. No more night shifts and much less fighting between my siblings. I was quietly overjoyed! But as with most things in life, a new challenge presented itself. Our financial struggle became even more evident to others around us. At this point, I could only assume out of sheer desperation, my mum started to date this guy who used to hang around at a nearby corner shop. From my quick and uneducated assessment back then, he was a downright alcoholic. I guess, at the time, he provided some level of assistance, but he scared the shit out of me. Many times, I hid and cried secretly after they would have a huge argument, because it always seemed to escalate so quickly; too often becoming physical. I remember praying so hard to God that this man not kill my mum, often confessing that I would never again complain about not having enough of anything. I just wanted him gone from around our family.

The situation became so volatile during this phase in my life that I was afraid to even close my eyes. Even with my mum beside me, I was terrified to go to sleep at night. Furthermore, most evenings, I would walk home from school with my siblings, and their friends but would always take off running and leaving them behind from the time we cleared the lonely part of the track. My sole mission was to arrive home as quickly as possible to ensure my mum was still alive. This situation continued for a few months until, one evening, I ran into the worst sight of my life. My mum's boyfriend had her pinned down in the backyard and was beating her unmercifully. I just stood there, completely helpless, and in a state of shock. After a few minutes, in an almost comatose state, I found the courage to scream and run back out the house straight to the corner shop and pleaded with the gentlemen there to come save my mum. Thankfully, two guys managed to pull him off and temper his rage before he disappeared. That evening, I recall my house being a disaster zone. The police, my gran who was in a rage, and the entire neighborhood had gathered; many lingering around for quite a while. A few days later, my mum was up and moving around again, albeit with a slight limp. She sat my siblings and I down on the table and explained to us that she was sorry for risking our lives and scaring us the way she did. My mum further explained that despite the fear she felt in her heart for her life and our lives, she knew she needed to take the risk of engaging him in an argument, otherwise she feared that the situation would have ended a lot more fatal. My mum risked her own life that day to break us away from that maniac.

Subconsciously, I wondered whether this event that kept surfacing in my mind influenced my strong aversion to taking risks. While I may have been too young to understand everything, I did see their relationship as an obstacle to our happiness. I failed to understand why my mother would take such a huge risk to engage in a situation she could not control or where the environment was not set up to play out in her favor. As young as I was back then, I remember feeling like her actions were totally reckless and irresponsible.

Overcoming Obstacles

"Obstacles are just opportunities dressed up as distractions; Allow yourself to see beyond the horizon."

I do not recall where I first heard the saying "obstacles present new opportunities," but these words have encapsulated my general approach to life. From an incredibly young age, I had already accepted that life will always throw us curveballs, but it was our duty to find ways to keep pressing forward. One thing was certain: I remained committed to removing any obstacles or behaviors that could hamper my personal life plans.

One of my strongest attributes over the years became the ability to see beyond the initial obstacles while actively searching for new opportunities. In retrospect, while I could always visualize the desired outcome, my aversion to taking risk was the only factor that many times crippled my ability to act or make speedy decisions. Early in my career, I often found myself going off on these extended fact-finding missions to mitigate the level of perceived risk. Over time, the ability to embrace a new approach to managing risk was very much tied to my desire to succeed. This deep-rooted desire to succeed caused me to maintain a positive attitude and mindset with laser-like focus on removing obstacles that can adversely impact the ability to pursue my dreams.

Stay Focused on the Prize!

At seventeen years old, I had my first major setback. Having achieved initial success in my Business Studies Certificate at the Samuel Jackman Prescod Polytechnic, a local skills development center, I was eager to further my education by pursuing a first-degree program. I recall being so excited when I got accepted to the University of the West Indies and Humber College in Canada. Sadly, that excitement was short lived since my father was evidently not eager to help fund my education, and my mum certainly could not afford it. I recall overhearing my mum's pleas to my father for help, but the end result remained unfavorable. What was a girl to do?

After days of tears and outright depression, while all my old classmates were soon jetting off to university, I realized I had to pull myself together and start searching for viable alternatives. I needed to devise a new course of action, because I was by no means prepared to allow this setback to completely ruin the overarching vision I had set for my life. I needed to "make something of myself," whatever that term really meant to me at the time. Clearly, adopting a doom and gloom mentally was not going to help me get back on track. I needed to understand and start pursuing other alternatives so that I could come up with a new game plan.

After weeks of aggressively mailing job applications, my mum saw the overall disappointment I was facing and invited me to tag along with her one Saturday to assist with some cleaning. Luckily for me, God was again working in my favor. The owner of the house happened to be a senior banker and after one conversation where I shared my dreams with him, he offered to help. I started assisting him on weekends with some bookkeeping, which I truly enjoyed, and over time had landed me a job, albeit a temporary attachment at Barclays Bank where my career really got started.

By the end of the first quarter of 2020, I had concluded that this year did not come to play. Having started out the year with a degree of intensity in my schedule that was by no means sustainable, I ended up lying on my back for over three weeks with the most excruciating migraines I had ever experienced. Then, along came the dreaded COVID-19 pandemic, which apparently did not want me to meet any of the personal or professional goals I had set for myself at the beginning of the year. Ironically, after doing a quick scan of my key goals with the hope of refining, I realized that I was only on track to finish reading the Book of Proverbs, in the Bible which by the way captures some really insightful words of wisdom. At that point, I was quite certain the universe was sending me a message. The reality was that the pandemic presented a mammoth obstacle that made getting back on track with any of my personal goals appear near impossible. For anything sensible to come of this year, it would certainly require me to shift my mindset while drawing heavily on my discipline and resilience. With signs of a new normal starting to emerge, it was time to stop wallowing in all the drama and negativity that was happening around me or in the news and refocus.

In my position as Director, I was working more intensely at home to resolve daily challenges presented by the pandemic while constantly working with my team to revamp operational action plans. Nevertheless, I soon realized that the extra time gained as a result of not having to commute was a gift that needed to be leveraged. I therefore got started on compiling all the content from my Personal Blog that could be used to create the manuscript for my book of life lessons. Before I knew it, I had something that was shaping up to be a first draft, which was all the motivation needed to keep going. I was again reminded that despite the severity of any situation, setbacks allow us time to refocus, remembering that life is really all about perspective.

As you continue to evolve, it is a given that you will encounter new challenges that will test and even change your original course of thinking, your plans, and core specific actions. Your level of success, however, will be very much dependent on how flexible you are to changing circumstances and how prepared you are to look beyond the horizon. Remember always "that if you find a path without any obstacles, it probably doesn't lead anywhere" (Frank A. Clark).

Building Capacity

"Transformation begins with you . . ."

I have always seen the value that comes from exhibiting a passion for continuous improvement of self, the team, and business products/services and processes when working to successfully execute a company's vision or seeking to transform organizational culture. Despite the intensity of my career over the years, it is evident that I somehow thrive on the adrenaline that comes from pushing past established boundaries, creating new innovations, and recording strong financial results all the while developing future leaders. Make no mistake, my ability to preserve a suitable work-life balance while pursuing my professional aspirations has often been comprised.

I recall after literally operating at lightning bolt pace for four consecutive years, I had declared that 2019 had to be an easier year for me. Almost instantly, one of my team members took the opportunity to point out that I make this same declaration every year, which really set me thinking. I do not have to tell you, this really was a true representation of my professional journey. Year after year, I somehow managed to thrive while going after both personal and professional goals that required me to push past what most would consider to be "established" boundaries.

Growth Sometimes Hurts; but Never Lose Sight of the Goal!

An important aspect of personal and professional growth is the ability to cultivate greater capacity. Unfortunately, many times, the opportunities presented will come in the form of problems in our personal lives and or new challenges in the business environment. Without such challenges, however, we would fail to acquire the skills of tenacity and resilience needed to build important coping techniques. The ability to overcome such challenges helps to strengthen our core and more adequately reposition our thinking and mindset for the future. It most certainly never feels that way at the time, but these unwelcomed and uncomfortable growth situations help us to build new levels of capacity and stamina without us even realizing it. Whether it be a new job, a tense working relationship with your manager or peers, juggling your career and academic studies, navigating a stressful personal relationship, or dealing with grief and even betrayal from a loved one, the ability to deal with life's challenges will help you emerge stronger as a true testament of our resilience while building new capacity levels each and every time.

While I had the benefit of working closely with senior management for many years, I also had the painstaking experience of working with my first female boss since reaching management level back in 2007. As a woman leader myself, I can assure you it disturbs me greatly to express this statement and the other observations that follow. The visible insecurities displayed by my then boss started to quickly create a toxic work environment, which over time created a myriad of challenges. Without realizing it at the time, her lack of competence in so many areas saw me being frequently invited to have a seat at the table for important strategic planning discussions and business meetings. A couple months into the role, my boss had initiated a new organizational structure that saw the entire team of business managers with responsibility for product development and marketing strategy whom I previously supported exiting the business. Believe me when I tell you, this period proved to be one of my greatest career challenges of all time; yet, it can easily be considered one of my most defining career moments to date.

As a newlywed at the time, my poor husband endured the brunt of my frustrations as he listened attentively to my ongoing rants at the end of each workday. For two years, my professionalism was not only being tested but overstretched on so many levels. Ironically, during this time, my capacity to learn, grow, and lead people more effectively had also increased to great proportions, all the while causing me to develop robust coping skills and mechanisms. Amid daily adversity, I naturally started to garner the trust and support of my team and wider colleagues. Truthfully, the more respect I gained as the informal leader, the more challenging my relationship with my boss became due to her insecurities and lack of self-confidence.

Despite the frustration and intensity of this period, I was truly inspired and determined not to fail nor buckle under the pressure. As the lead subject matter expert, my sole mission was to focus on delivering the unit's strategic goals. Based on my own struggles, I realized how important it was to continually shield the rest of my team from our boss' relentless pressures and, at times, senseless emotional outbursts. Things were so intense that during the first trimester of my pregnancy, my husband was extremely worried about me going to work in such a toxic and stressful environment.

Even though I had mastered the art of bottling my emotions in order to maneuver and maintain high performance standards despite the craziness that existed, his concerns were reasonable and warranted since we were actively trying to conceive for some time. He had over time come to the conclusion that our issues were my body's reaction to operating in the prolonged stressful environment. Admittedly, while this was a period of tremendous professional growth for me, the thought was constantly at the forefront of my mind that my sanity was way more important and maybe it was time for me to move on. However, mustering the courage to leave my team at such an unsettling time was pretty much unthinkable. I therefore made a conscious decision that I would continue to embrace the challenges presented while embracing the opportunity to learn and grow. I had pretty much made up in my mind that there was no way I was going to allow this situation to derail the vision I had envisioned for my life or the personal brand I had worked so hard to build prior to my boss's arrival.

Quite frankly, that entire experience had undoubtedly affected my perspective on women in leadership while helping to shape my own leadership style. Leaders who display insecurities and irrational thinking while leading a team can prove detrimental to even the best organizational cultures. In the midst of adversity, this experience helped me to adopt heightened levels of self-awareness as I became more intentional on "what not to do" as a business leader in order to positively influence the team and our ability to deliver strong results. Furthermore, this experience also taught me that there is little value in running away from the challenges presented throughout your career. Your best bet is always to grow through the situation as best you can, which will prove quite useful in the long run.

Feedback as a Recipe for Success

"The single best piece of advice I can offer right from the start is to always assume there is room for improvement in everything you do."

When we are in growth mode, all feedback should be considered good feedback; and yes, even the bits that are tough for us to hear at times. We cannot change what we are not aware of, so the journey to success must include timely and candid feedback. The reality however is that there is always room for improvement, so we must maintain an open mind while embracing the feedback provided, if it is to be effective. Ken Blanchard said, "feedback is the breakfast of champions!" The practice of listening with the aim of understanding and not simply to respond or offer excuses is difficult to master but absolutely necessary for our continued professional development.

Treat Feedback as a Gift and Not a Slap in the Face!

Creating a feedback loop that forces you to constantly evaluate your own performance is an excellent place to start. To really see the benefits of this approach, however, you must be prepared to take your head out of the clouds and ask yourself how well you handled that last situation, prepared that last report, or delivered that last presentation. This can go a long way in helping you identify your strengths and weaknesses and thus prove to be a winning recipe for success.

Another technique adopted by some businesses as part of their continuous improvement strategy is to conduct a SWOT analysis aimed at identifying the strengths, weaknesses, opportunities, and threats faced by the company. This model holds true at a personal level as well and would be another great place to start, if you are looking to reposition your personal brand, create a greater impact, or simply realign your overall performance.

One of the simplest yet most powerful tools you can explore as part of your growth strategy is a Personal Development Assessment. The objective of such an assessment is to identify any performance gaps or areas that may require your immediate attention. This can be in the form of an easy to execute digital survey that incorporates three core components: your own personal view of your performance, feedback from a few selected peers, and your leader's perspective. For this tool to be truly effective, you must be mentally prepared to take action upon presentation of the findings. Many people have a view of their performance that can vary significantly from the perception of others. I once heard the saying that mistakes should be examined, learned from, and discarded, not dwelled upon and stored. We all know it is never a good feeling when we make mistakes or when others highlight our weakness, but it does provide a perfect opportunity for us to learn and grow.

As a new manager, I quickly understood the importance of obtaining feedback coming out of my first performance review as a member of the management team. The move from supervisor to management not only came with greater responsibility but significantly increased expectations. Despite achieving all the unit's performance goals that year, I somehow left my performance review feeling like a complete failure. Ironically, while I was working to meet the set department goals, my leader was expecting me take on a more strategic leadership role and to be more proactive in finding creative ways and developing plans on how the department could be reformed. How was I supposed to know that? And wouldn't that present a conflict if I overstepped my boundaries? What were my boundaries, anyway? These were just a few of the questions that surfaced in my mind as I left the meeting, feeling like I did not deliver, despite my noticeable and significant contribution.

Of course, this feedback sent me in a tailspin! I was floored, and it honestly took me off my game for a couple days. Nevertheless, as part of my commitment to succeed in the role, I picked myself up and arranged a follow up meeting with my manager. Understanding the expectations of me for the future was burning at the forefront of my mind. At that point, I had recommitted to always function at a level that adds more value than required, which proved to be a winning strategy that quickly fueled my career advancement. During this period of self-doubt as a young manager, I discovered how useful having a good mentor could be to support your professional growth. The people that see the potential in you before you see it in yourself are always the best to have around. Mentorship can take a formal or informal structure but, either way, the relationship should provide you with honest and candid feedback, along with clear suggestions that aid the way you navigate situations in today's constantly changing and fast-paced environment. Some mentors can turn out to be great, long-lasting friends, but the best mentors are persons who care for you and believe in you and yet remain capable of being a true mentor first and friend second.

Embracing feedback as part of your commitment to ongoing learning and development must remain part of your future growth strategy. The icing on the cake is finding yourself a really good mentor who is equally committed to helping you succeed in both your personal and professional growth, while offering that much-needed inspiration through their own actions and progress.

Claim Your Seat
at the Table

*"Don't try to stay where you are or once were
to make others comfortable. Let your growth
challenge everyone and everything around you!"*

—Sarah Jake-Roberts

As I reflected on International Women's Day this year, under the theme "EachforEqual," I was absolutely marveled by the level of progress women leaders all over the world have made in advancing their careers and personal agendas while influencing a wide cross section of people through the power of their voices. We have really stepped it up a notch so kudos to womanpower and our continued progress. Closer to home in Barbados, we have our first government administration that includes eight dynamic, powerful, and impactful women bosses, including our very own Honorable Prime Minister and Governor General. Yet despite all this progress, most boardrooms today are dominated by the opposite sex. It is no wonder there is so much buzz about gender equality and women empowerment rights. All I know is that the time has come for us to see more women leaders in the boardroom but I passionately believe that this change is within our power to make. In my view, this is not a gender issue. Our progress will be determined by how much time we invest in both our professional and personal development and, more importantly, how we as women continue to support each other. When I reflect on where I started, I have no doubt that this can be achieved.

I once had the extreme pleasure of attending an international forum with a distinguished panel that included a group of strong, fierce, determined, charismatic, dynamic, "badass" women, all leaders in their own respective fields, who shared their personal stories. The energy in the room was surreal, and I was truly energized and inspired being around so many impressive women leaders. For the first time in a long time, I felt like I was right where I belonged and was moved to tears as I imagined the pride my mum feels daily as she witnesses my efforts and passion to keep evolving.

My team recently asked me the most important message I could share with women thinking about advancing their careers. I hesitated initially, but only because I knew they would limit me to a specific word count, knowing that this is a topic I am extremely passionate about. With over twenty-two years as a seasoned career professional with regional experience and having always at the forefront of change in both my current and previous roles, I have acquired a wealth of knowledge, skills, and technical expertise that has influenced my leadership style and career advancement. That being said, my passion continues to truly lie in the people development element of leadership—the satisfaction that comes from watching others grow.

From my perspective, we must move rigorously to claim our seats at the table. Women leaders need to understand that there is no "easy" path to success. Our success will be very much defined by our commitment to continuous growth achieved through new learnings and our willingness to embrace new opportunities that cause us to stand out. For women to continue breaking new glass ceilings, we must definitely get used to being uncomfortable while adopting a can-do attitude and much greater self-awareness. It is time we realize that a positive attitude is a new Superpower that can get you into rooms, get you a seat at the table, and, if we are consistent, can keep us there. Sadly, this is one of the most challenging personal traits for some female professionals to adopt. Both our rise to success and sluggish professional growth can at times be affected by poor attitudes and unguarded emotions, which is manifested in our performance. I even shudder to mention this "I have arrived" mentally that appears to get switched on so easily when some women reach a certain level of success or status quo, often earning the rest of us ladies some really undesirable titles. I look forward to the day when woman enthusiastically help each other as we continue the fight for our seat at the table.

It is time to accept the promotion to "CEO of Your Life." If you are to continue lobbying for a seat at the table, you must be prepared to pause and come up with a career game plan that ties in with your passions. Once you have identified where you want to be in two years, five years, or even ten years, you must go about executing that plan with the highest degree of discipline that causes you to stand out amongst your peers. However, remember to remain flexible and know that if the chosen path comes without obstacles, it probably does not lead anywhere. Practicing daily gratitude shifts our mindset and fuels our hunger for success. It is therefore important that we remain truly thankful for all new opportunities presented.

If women are to continue claiming their seats at the table, the best advice I can offer is simply to show up, but do so daily with a positive attitude and filled with sufficient passion that exudes confidence, self-belief, and excellence in everything you do. Remembering that consistency breeds results, results bring success, and success delivers rewards.

Stay Committed to Helping Others Grow

"When you have worked hard and done well and walked through that door of opportunity, do not slam it shut behind you. Reach back and give others the same chances that helped you to succeed."

—Michelle Obama

After losing my grandmother on Christmas Day back in 2006, the holiday season is now a time of serious reflection for me. Not sure if it's the body or mind, but I seem much more willing to let myself pause and consider the things that truly matter in my life. In recent times, my passion for mentoring and coaching others continues to be top of mind. As a leader, I constantly seek to inspire, build confidence, empower, and encourage others to believe they too can achieve anything that they put their minds to. These powerful words of wisdom, spoken by one of the most—if not the most—inspirational and iconic female, First Lady Michelle Obama, have undoubtedly had a profound impact on me. More and more, I feel compelled to invest time to share and mentor others with the hope of influencing the decisions that take them one step closer to achieving their professional goals. Maya Angelou was on to something when she said, "as you grow older you will discover that you have two hands, one for helping yourself and the other for helping others."

This deep-rooted drive to inspire and motivate others to go after their dreams and reach their highest potential is what has led me to share my real-life experiences. The specific focus on developing soft skills was by no means accidental. Time and time again, it is being highlighted by business leaders that these important personal qualities and skills are lacking within today's workforce. This skills gap is holding many persons back from reaching their optimal level of professional growth and career advancement, even employees who have great potential. Zig Ziglar suggests that "a lot of people have gone further than they thought they could because someone else believed they could."

My most gratifying experiences as a business leader thus far has been watching others grow and blossom into well-rounded, driven, and passionate professionals, knowing that I had a hand in shaping their career journey. As leaders, it is important that we remain committed to the professional development of those under our care while mastering the art of providing timely feedback and encouragement. Staying committed to helping others take their performance to the next level augurs well toward building more impactful and successful leaders. It is the leader's duty to help others unleash the hidden talent that will allow them to reach their fullest potential.

Not Always an Easy Road

Leading or mentoring people is by no means a walk in the park. How do you successfully convince others to see what you see in them or at least to visualize themselves a couple years down the road? This right here is the true leadership challenge and, quite frankly, can come with much frustration but as leaders we must remain committed to the mission. Fostering strong relationships with individual team members is paramount to achieving any real success. Employees need to know that you genuinely care about them before they place their trust in your intentions. Once the trust has been established, you are more likely to have an impact on employees with a growth mindset. In contrast, team members with a fixed mindset will require a daily dose of energy and reaffirmation of leadership purpose if the leader is to continue to make any real strides in getting these employees to see and take positive action.

There is no doubt that this can be frustrating for leaders, but we don't have the luxury of throwing our hands up in the air. If you genuinely wish to see employees move to the next level, then you must be prepared to have those candid conversations while creating a practical, proactive action plan geared toward affecting real change.

The Trust Factor

There is no single approach or secret weapon I can recommend for uncapping the potential or hidden talent you see in others. John C. Maxwell reminds us that "as leaders, we must be close enough to inspire and far enough to offer candid feedback." From my experience, leaders who are not genuinely people-oriented or overly introverted tend to struggle to build trust and consistency in their efforts at helping others to grow. In contrast, the sad reality is that there are many insecure leaders out there, which contributes to toxic work environments. These types of bosses are more concerned about their own job security than helping others reach their fullest potential. Holding back important information or sidelining key team members out of the decision-making process are just a few of the strategies deployed by these type of bosses. Having experienced this firsthand, I can say that this really should not be classified as leadership since it only stifles the true potential of others.

Leadership is all about people. Authentic leadership calls for leaders to be vulnerable, and sometimes the best way to influence and inspire others is to share our own personal stories. Practicing the art of "storytelling" as a leadership tool helps you to connect and show employees that they too can accomplish their goals. The role of a leader is to inspire, embolden, empower, and encourage others to believe they can achieve anything they put their minds to, supported by a degree of discipline. Staying committed to helping others create meaningful growth plans that help shape both their personal and professional journey is the trademark of successful leadership. Will you always get it right? Will you successfully make this connection with every team member? Not at all, but the ability to spot potential in others and successfully inspire them enough to take any real action is a truly remarkable experience.

From a Leader's Perspective

"Always remember life is a journey and the best leaders are those that bring their authentic self to the table, while sharing and connecting with others."

*E*xperience has taught me that good leadership, above all else, is crucial to driving organizational success. As a leader, you are in the spotlight at all times so your performance matters. While the debate on whether leaders are born or made continues, one thing I can assure you is that leadership truly is about the ability to positively influence others. More so, a fundamental objective of effective leadership must be development of the team, as part of the overall process. Ultimately, the true test of a great leader is in the ability to inspire and motivate others. John C. Maxwell offer a simple definition: "Leadership is the ability to influence others, nothing more, nothing less." *Leadership is all about people and, truthfully, it is easier when you genuinely care.*

Several scenarios presented to me during 2018 caused me to pause and reflect on the importance of good leadership in order to drive organizational success. Let me assure you, striking a balance between focusing on profitability and ongoing development of the team presents a constant challenge for many business leaders, myself included. Often, the inability to identify with a clear purpose, coupled with the lack of emotional intelligence, presents a real challenge for either the leader, team members, or both.

Leadership requires you to always remain optimistic, even with the path to success remains unclear. The most effective leaders are those who manage to remain positive even in the face of adversity. The importance of acquiring such leadership skills must be emphasized. As the formal or informal leader, one must become self-aware, which would allow for better self-management. Realizing how your actions, reactions, and overall demeanor impacts others will go a long way in developing critical leadership skills. Another important point worth highlighting is that while leadership can be quite rewarding, it comes with a great deal of personal sacrifice. Without a doubt, a great degree of brain power and resilience is needed if you are to effectively sustain your leadership effectiveness.

In 2011, I took on a new leadership role that required me to focus my efforts on changing an existing organizational culture as a fundamental strategy to realigning the business' performance. The benefits derived from consistency in my leadership style and strategic thinking cannot be overemphasized during that time of transformation. An important observation that my previous leadership experience had taught me was that you must be close enough to relate to others but far enough ahead to motivate them if you see tangible results. The most effective leaders are those who place people at the forefront of the journey, creating a culture of high employee engagement, fueled by continuous improvement of self, processes, and the company's products or services.

The real challenge for today's leaders, however, is that this constantly calls for a serious balancing act. One of my most rewarding experiences as a leader was back in 2016. During that year, the team had worked feverishly on the development and launch of a new Visa Credit Card product in the Barbados market, making the business the first non-financial institution in the English-speaking Latin America Caribbean (LAC) Region to successfully obtain a Visa Member Principal License. The intensity of project deliverables that year was high but so was the energy within the team. Every single day, week, and month saw a new challenge being presented. Thankfully, the team was more than ready to take it on.

Five years later, we had managed to successfully transform the culture which happened to be a key success factor during this important strategic project. After working for almost a year without a break, and never once complaining, my team was ready for product launch. I recall September 26, 2016, being such an emotional day for me. Not only was the launch event a resounding success but also witnessing the pride, joy, and comradery among the team and our leaders as we celebrated our success brought me to tears that night.

Leadership Requires Continuous Learning

"Personal Growth Equals Opportunity."

*D*uring my teenage years, I really struggled to keep up with my studies. This was not at all due to lack of effort, but unlike many of my classmates, I realized that I needed to study hard if I were to consistently achieve good grades. With no one in my family to offer any academic support, I simply had to buckle down and put in the extra work. Interestingly, I always performed quite well with practical assignments and, truth be told, I honestly think this is what secured my future in banking.

Due to financial constraints, I did not go to University to pursue my first degree, and my High School Mathematics Grade could easily be described as average. This presented a challenge for me at the bank during the performance evaluation process that would determine my transition from part-time to full-time employment status. As I waited for the Human Resources Department to make a final decision, I recall going home to my mum crying every evening during that period of uncertainty.

Thankfully, despite my failure to meet the banking requirements, the Managing Director had put forward a strong recommendation in support of my continued service in a full-time capacity based solely on the work ethic, dedication, and commitment shown in my first year. This victory changed my life, as this job was super important to me. I saw it as the perfect opportunity for me to jumpstart the vision I had created for my life, coupled with my eagerness to help my mum in a greater way financially. During that very unsettling period, one thing became certain. I realized that no matter how hard I worked and how good I was at the job, I would always need to focus on personal development. That same semester, I enrolled myself into an evening program to further my Business Studies at our local Community College. The ultimate sacrifice of leaving classes around nine at night and taking the long, lonely journey home on the bus was indeed worthwhile. My ability to blend the knowledge acquired during the program with my practical experience truly helped to boost my confidence and on the job performance. In many instances, I was the only student in the class with a full-time job, which made my contribution more valuable to my lecturer and classmates, who quickly started to look at me for feedback and guidance. I quickly became intrigued with the concept of management and leadership and continued to apply this knowledge to my advantage in my business environment.

In a previous chapter, I spoke of the importance of having a personal growth plan if you are serious about achieving career success. For anyone currently leading a team or desirous of leading a team in the near future, your professional development should never be taken for granted. Your ability to add real value comes from the knowledge and guidance you can offer the team and your leaders. My own journey toward continuous learning saw me reading every management book I could get my hands on, with John C. Maxwell and Steven Covey being my go-to business authors. The more I functioned within the corporate world, the more curious I became about leadership. Having the benefit of working with both good and bad managers over the years, I consciously adopted the practice of filtering the behaviors I did not desire to have influence my own leadership attributes.

On our career journey, we must always be prepared to grow on all fronts. In 2018, I had the extreme privilege of attending the Ivey Business School in London, Ontario. During the morning of the first day of class, I literally pinched myself because it felt like a dream. All I could think of was how proud my grandmother and mother must be! I was again back in a classroom but this time among a cohort of CEOs, COOs, CFOs, Presidents, Vice Presidents and Senior Directors. I do not think anyone could have prepared me for the intensity of the program. With a daily class schedule from Monday and Saturday 8:00 a.m. to 9:30 p.m. with nightly 40–50-page case study prep for the next morning, I swear the program was literally a two-year MBA program crammed into three weeks. The strategic knowledge imparted throughout the program was phenomenal, but the most rewarding aspect for me was the self-evaluation session with an assigned Personal Coach. His job was to share with me his professional assessment of my group participation during a number of activities, culminating with the findings from my 360 Degree Leadership Assessment, which was completed by my boss, peers, and direct reports. I guess the Program Managers knew that many experienced leaders at this level were not at all that good at embracing feedback. I, however, was totally prepared for whatever comments were captured in the report, since I have always seen the value of feedback as part of my continuous improvement strategy. I openly confided in my Coach about my experiences and areas of anxiousness because, trust me, being at the top can be lonely at times. It was great to have a stranger who came prepared to listen and offer unbiased feedback on the areas where I needed to pay closer attention.

As you climb the leadership ladder, the ability to gain a greater level of self-awareness through feedback will prove paramount to the sustainability of your journey. The willingness to embrace feedback that identifies areas of strength and weakness will go a long way to improving your overall performance and career success. In this volatile, uncertain, complex, and ambiguous (VUCA) world we now live in, adopting the practice of intentional learning and continuous improvement of self truly is a strategic way to set yourself apart.

If there is one thing experience has taught me, it is that every advance you make along your career journey will require a shift to your way of thinking. To be an effective leader, you must first be prepared to become a leader to yourself before you can lead others. Your efforts to stay ahead of the game will allow you to continually add meaningful value to your leaders, peers, direct reports, customers, professional network, and the communities you serve.

Leading in Times of Crisis

"In the middle of difficulty lies opportunities."

—Albert Einstein

Now more than ever, I am convinced that God has been preparing me for this leadership journey my entire life. Over the years, ongoing health trials and other personal obstacles threatened to derail my career progress, but the good Lord was somehow always in my corner. My resilience and perseverance were stronger than I could ever comprehend and, many times, the only way that I could rationalize my progress was to accept that I am a child of God.

This was again tested in March 2020, when the novel coronavirus (COVID-19) hit the shores of Barbados. I had literally just returned to work after a prolonged flare up of cluster and migraine headaches when the rapid escalation of a three-phase national plan that our Government had outlined sent me on a tailspin. The country moved from planning to implementation at lightning speed, leaving most businesses scampering and grappling with serious holes in their business continuity plans; my business was no exception. My first priority was to work with the team to prepare an outline of our contingency plan even though many elements remained untested. My core planning team and I were literally tweaking and changing on the fly as this crisis was by no means considered part of our existing business continuity plan. Never did I imagine leading a business during a time that would see a virus move to cripple powerful countries with major resources at their disposal, bring striving industries to a halt, question the future of global companies, and make it all the way to our shores in Barbados. These were definitely unprecedented times.

The complexity of managing through a crisis requires leaders to successfully juggle complex demands, which can be extremely challenging for leaders who are expected to provide a variety of timely decisions and responses. Common leadership approaches may not work in the face of adversity, so leaders must remain open-minded to new perspectives, which at times can come from within the team if a culture of creative thinking and collaboration exist. Imagine leading during a time where sound logic, methodical thinking, and a solid communication strategy became irrelevant based on the swift escalation of changing circumstances within the country. The harsh reality of this crisis was that our plans of yesterday were null and void for tomorrow. We were forced daily to expand our creative thinking to ensure that the business had a Plan A, B, C, and D! And even then, we were still caught off guard in some areas. As a services company, our customer communication strategy was crucial, as in times of crisis and panic, the obvious is not so obvious anymore. Simplification in messaging was the order of the day. As Director, my days were long and intense, filled with endless planning meetings, networking to address issues that occasionally needed government intervention, all the while juggling rapid responses to my core planning team that would allow the team to maintain momentum. Admittedly, I was still not back to optimal health, and the luxury of a good night's sleep was simply not afforded to me during those first few weeks of managing the crisis. My mind was constantly racing as I reflected on the day's progress, the plans of tomorrow, and the recovery strategies that would help to minimize the impact of the crisis and effects it would have on the team and the future of our business operations.

My own leadership effectiveness played on my mind. I wondered whether I was lending sufficient support to the team, since I was considered high risk and therefore working remotely. I recall my first call on mornings was to my Operations Manager to pick up where we left off or to share any new thoughts, insights, or discuss the actions required. Her support during this crisis became my saving grace as we continued to rally around each other. I was reminded daily that leaders are only as good as the team their surround themselves with.

There was no playbook for managing through the crisis, and I was forced to rely heavily on my strategic leadership foundation and critical thinking skills. All I knew was that I absolutely needed to show up and deliver a strong performance, because our ability to survive and thrive beyond this crisis sat squarely on my shoulders. The buck stopped with me, and I was by no means prepared to fail nor compromise the livelihoods of the team. We had no choice but to come out on the other side of this crisis, albeit with a few invaluable lessons. From offering updates to operational plans, to actively monitoring cash flows, to our resource management strategy, this crisis saw a new level of thinking and collaboration. The team was forced to leverage trust for each other and teamwork in order to survive the constantly changing operational models as this continued for weeks with every new amendment to the country's health and safety curfew orders. I was well aware that my performance was constantly being assessed at all levels. My CEO and the wider executive team were relying on me to successfully navigate the business through these uncharted waters. Meanwhile, my team was expecting me to clear the path of any major obstacles, while providing active guidance in support of every changing circumstances.

During this challenging period, my passion for continuous learning coupled with the desire to bring us out of this crisis intact led me to tune into several webinars with subject matter experts. During a session focused on *Leading Through A Crisis* hosted by the John C. Maxwell Team, I found myself reflecting on the leadership concept of *Pain-Gain-Experience (PGE)* that was highlighted. PGE simply suggests that there are three stages a leader goes through when leading in a crisis. But this set me thinking, was this really a new leadership concept? The concept suggests that, first, you will encounter pain as you maneuver the crisis; this same pain allows you to gain some valuable lessons and even enhance or acquire new skills, which ultimately adds to your wealth of experiences. For me, this model seemed relevant to anyone seeking to take their life to the next level.

It is proven time and time again that when we are in the moment, we tend not to focus on anything else but the pain. However, during this pandemic, this was a luxury not afforded to leaders. With the understanding that uncertainty naturally creates panic, effective leadership required that you remain the "calm" and be the "voice of reason" in the storm if the team was to pull through the crisis. Being effective in your leadership requires you to lead from the front, while knowing when to scale back and allow others to do their part. The best leaders understand the importance of genuinely connecting with their people, and more so during a crisis. No one expects you to have all the answers, yet as leaders we must show up and exhibit optimism all the way, inspiring belief that our people will pull through. As difficult as it may be, leading through any crisis (far less the COVID-19 pandemic, where it literally looked and felt like the entire world was falling apart), requires leaders to see beyond the horizon. The leader's role is to see the opportunities, set the strategic plans in motion and inspire hope! Creativity, strategic thinking, calm, empathy, and steadiness must become your trademark if you are to effectively steer the ship to safer waters, giving birth to a new level of resilience.

Managing through the COVID-19 crisis was highly intense and often daunting, to say the least but quiet resolve was the order of the day. My capacity and resilience were being tested daily; yet, tenacity and drive to actively overcome the challenges as they were presented was the only remedy in the leadership survival tool kit. In reflection, I had the good fortune of working with a highly dedicated and flexible team, including a new, incredibly talented Operations Manager who I had hired a few months prior to the crisis. Again, I was reminded of God's glory and his way of always blessing me with just what I need at the right time throughout my leadership journey.

The Balancing Act

"The Struggle Is Real."

The climb up the corporate ladder comes with its fair share of personal sacrifices. As you advance throughout your career, the growing demands on your time can certainly make it difficult to truly unplug. The quest to cultivate greater capacity, which will be essential for career progress, needs to be balanced with adequate levels of self-care. As a career professional, mother, and wife, I am constantly fighting to strike the right balance and, truth be told, there are times when I fail miserably. With this new world order that we live in, there seems to be a default expectation (sometimes self-imposed) to always be switched on, which poses a real challenge for persons to truly disconnect and recharge.

I once had a boss who would send emails very late into the night with specific requests and then appear at my desk before 7:30 a.m. the next day to ask me whether I saw his email and proceed to ask for updates. The sad reality is that I used to read and start to action the emails. During that phase in my life, I had adopted the practice of resuming work late in the evenings after I had managed to get my two-year-old settled in bed. But the audacity for him to have the expectation so early in the morning? Thankfully, I was also at the stage in my career where I understood the importance of managing my leader's expectations, by under-promising and over-delivering.

Almost Everything Will Work Again If You Unplug It, Including You!

One of the most significant areas of compromise as we juggle the demands of going after a corporate career happens to be our health, mental state, and relationships. Striking a balance that allows you the room to take care of yourself and your loved ones without feeling guilty, in my view, is a significant milestone. Elevated levels of stress associated with maneuvering through the corporate rigours continues to be the underlying cause of many health-related problems.

I recall a period of intensity in my life where I was literally living out of a suitcase due to my regional role at the bank. Between the long hours, the delayed flights, the business meetings, the reports due for submission, and the project calls, I was on the verge of burn out and I knew it. My body was sending me all sorts of signals that I needed to slow down. Due to everyone's expectations of me as the leader and subject matter expert, I pushed ahead and continued ignoring the signs until one night while on a business trip in Jamaica.

Shortly after collecting my dinner from the buffet station and heading back to my table, I sat there over my plate unable to breathe, unable to move, and unable to attract anyone's attention to seek help. Fortunately, one of my colleagues staying at the hotel while on a different assignment came over to greet me. Quickly realizing I was in distress, she jumped into action. I recall being rushed to the hospital and being placed on drips, nebulizer, and the full works. The entire experience still seems surreal when I think about it. I ended up staying in Jamaica for almost a week beyond my original departure date with no family and a new asthma diagnosis at the age of twenty-seven.

The Power of Pause

You will find that your career advancement brings greater demands on your time, which presents a real balancing act. As you reach a certain level of leadership, delegation, discipline, and mastering the art of tactfully saying "no" will be paramount to sustaining the balance required for preserving a more desirable quality of life. Sometimes, we get so busy focusing on our careers or simply striving to maintain the performance standards set for ourselves or expected by others that we forget self-care requires discipline too. Developing a routine that allows you to pause, reset, and refuel our mind, body, and soul is crucial to sustaining high-performance standards. The power of pause allows us to deliver the best version of ourselves, which over time leads to a more satisfying life and sustainable performance. Spending quality time with family, developing an exercise routine, finding time to spend with yourself and those in your inner circle, journaling, meditating, getting adequate levels of sleep, incorporating a balanced diet, enjoying the nature around us, and enjoying spa treatments all positively impact our daily effectiveness. The saying *"you can't pour from an empty cup"* becomes even more relevant when balancing a demanding career or on a mission to achieve career success.

Over time, I have come to realize that the same effort placed on pursuing your career goals is required to build an effective self-care regime. Being intentional about pre-booking self-care appointments and penciling in exercise, some alone time, and blocking out a lunch hour are all ways that you can start to maintain proper balance. My workdays are full of meetings, so the one thing I have learned over the years is that meal prep allows me to maintain a much better diet. Plus, with so many new apps out there to help us manage some of these activities, we really have little excuse for not doing a better job of taking care of ourselves, myself included. But as with most things in life, you will sometimes go off track (believe me, I know).

Practicing good self-care definitely requires an intentional approach. Personally, the anticipation of connecting with a girlfriend for a couple of drinks or knowing that I will soon be jetting off on my annual family vacation as a means of distressing is invaluable. No longer do shopping trips attract me, but I am always game for a fun girls' trip or family vacation.

You must find what works for you and try to strike that much-needed balance, never neglecting that your spirit will also need refueling at times.

Embrace the Journey

"Whenever you are prepared to level up, know that it's going to get tough. But you've got this!"

During the preceding chapters, my goal was simply to highlight that growth is an evolving process, so you absolutely have to keep moving. Denzel Washington once shared with a group of graduating students, "dreams without goals are just dreams!" while the late Kobe Bryant argued that "great things only come from hard work and perseverance; no excuses." These profound statements symbolize my approach taken to building career success over the years. While many have ascribed me with the title of workaholic, I continue to accept the real fact that given where I started, nothing I have achieved in this life would have been possible without my commitment to putting in the work. I therefore truly understand and can relate to the important life lessons being imparted by both these great icons. It is highly unlikely that you would find any successful person saying that the journey to pursuing their dreams, and ultimately success, was a simple one; achieved without activating an intentional game plan supported by consistency and discipline. Almost certainly, the immediate response would be to highlight the number of sleepless nights and the sweat, tears, and relationships lost in pursuit of reaching their goals.

One day, not one but two of my team members said to me that they did not want to ever become a Director. After getting over my initial shock and disappointment, because both these individuals possess such great potential, I quickly realized that they get to see firsthand the demands of performing at executive level, the situations presented that I am required to maneuver daily, and the pace generally required to stay ahead of the game.

Of course, I would have been remiss not to share my perspective, since I am a firm believer that nothing worth having in this life tends to come easy. In the moment, the challenges faced in both our personal and professional lives can really throw us off our game, causing us to go through some really turbulent times. Over time, however, we come to realize that the struggles, frustrations, and disappointments become the foundation that helps to shape our future. These are all part of our personal story. The attitude and mindset adopted throughout our daily encounters is hands down what will fuel our ability to develop important coping skills that position us for long-term success. Through our daily actions and reactions, we are developing habits that highlight an attitude of gratitude for the opportunities that come our way, challenges included, or allowing fear of failure and frustrations to cause us to become stuck where we are. There is no easy, clearly marked path to personal success; success is an uphill journey that requires transformation. Michelle Obama describes transformation as a forward motion to become the best version of yourself.

"For me, becoming isn't about arriving somewhere or achieving a certain aim. I see it instead as forward motion, a means of evolving, a way to reach continuously towards a better self. The journey doesn't end!" **(Michelle Obama)**

Transformation is by no means an overnight process. Sustainable success comes to those truly prepared to embrace and endure the climb, with higher than normal levels of consistency and discipline. Transforming your life calls for you to constantly visualize your future self while being deliberate about becoming that person at every stage of the journey. This can sometimes result in lost friendships, a shift in focus from things you once fancied, and a myriad of new challenges. Yet, whenever you make a conscious decision to pursue your dreams, you must be truly prepared to confront the roadblocks that will be presented.

From my own experience, to successfully maneuver these sometimes turbulent waters, I needed to do things differently, constantly step outside of my comfort zone, tackle challenges head on, and embrace the fact that there is always something new to learn from each experience. I am sure you can all identify at least two or three goals you would love to achieve in this lifetime. For me, reaching a stage in my life where I would be an example to future generations or be in a position to reach back and pull others up continued to shape my future plans and is now the driving force in my execution.

At times, our personal goals can be quite scary due to the absence of a clear roadmap that shows us how to get started. But, as I like to say, without a start, there is no chance of ever finishing, so it would prove beneficial to buckle down, do some research on the chosen area of interest, apply your collective learnings, get your attitude and mindset in check, and just go ahead and get started. This mindset forces you to keep all your actions and reactions aligned toward the desired end state. Each level of your life will require a different you, so despite the roadblocks, you must always continue to trust the process. Walking into my first Board Meeting to represent a business did not just happen overnight but was certainly a testament to what is possible. You must believe in your abilities and deliver with a rigor of excellence and consistency that causes others to believe in you too. From experience, people tend to see the success stories and rarely acknowledge the struggles. Actively pursuing personal and/or professional goals calls for some serious personal sacrifice. The struggles are real! Regardless of your chosen journey, sustainable success will be determined by your work ethic, your passion, your drive, your integrity, and your personal standards of excellence, and most definitely not your title.

A growth mindset allows us to consistently see challenges, delays, and even setbacks as an opportunity to reassess the situation for a better comeback. These are what I like to refer to as "defining moments"; the points at which we rise to the occasion while building character, capacity, and tenacity. The mind is a powerful tool, and once we begin to rewire it correctly, we possess the potential to function on a whole new level. Based on my own personal experience, this has been proven true time and time again. The journey to success, whatever that looks like for you, is one that forces us to keep evolving. It is important that you chart a path forward for your life that aligns with your own dreams, passions, and deepest desires. Besides the gift of God's mercy, this has proven to be a source of constant motivation for me; that much-needed internal boost of energy that helps to get me back on track time after time.

Conclusion

"If you don't try to create the future you want, you must endure the future you get."

—John C. Maxwell

*T*hroughout the previous chapters of this book, I have shared some of my favorite quotes, but I could not have found a more appropriate quote to conclude my collection of Life Lessons. Having grown up in an environment where I watched my grandmother and mother fight daily to create a better life for the family, I too was prepared to put in the work required in pursuit of a better future, albeit choosing a different approach. Either ironically or as God's way to further instill the value of hard work in me, the words of my primary school motto "Nothing Is Gained without Hard Work" were firmly cemented in my brain from an early age. Having achieved a fulfilling career has shown me that, regardless of your beginnings, we all have the God given potential to go after the life we desire. The real opportunity before you comes from visualizing your future self, taking deliberate steps daily toward your chosen path, and focusing your efforts on always improving yourself while enforcing high personal standards with the understanding that your life only gets better when you do.

As a business leader, it is both challenging and frustrating at times to work with a generation with so much potential that has been wired with what I refer to as an "entitlement mentality." Far too many of our young professionals joining the workforce are failing to show commitment and consistency in their work ethics while displaying troubling levels of emotional intelligence. The prevalent misconception that the rise to the top will happen overnight and that academic accomplishments are the only recipes for success places this generation at a serious disadvantage. In the book *Good to Great,* Jim Collins discussed a statement made by one of the CEOs he interviewed. The highly successful Wall Street executive articulated how "he never stopped trying to become qualified for the job." This resonated with me on so many levels, because a huge part of my success at gaining a seat at the table over the years was due to my commitment and intentional efforts to always add meaningful value.

My excitement at the prospect of giving back to others through mentorship has ultimately influenced my decision to take the bold step of publishing this book. With so many opportunities before us as businesses continue to focus on digital transformation and continuous improvement through new product design or service innovations, the opportunities for young professionals are endless. Today's leaders are looking for positive, creative, assertive, hardworking, and solutions-driven team players to join their inner circle as they seek to retain their best talent. You must, however, be prepared to roll up your sleeves and get on with the important task of developing yourself. Taking the time to create a career game plan in support of your continued growth in all aspects of your life will prove beneficial in the long run. As the CEO of your life, you must certainly understand that your "attitude, mindset, and consistency" are paramount to your success. It really does not matter how good you are at what you do. If your mindset is not right and your attitude is off, you will probably struggle to reach or sustain high levels of performance. In a world where there are so many negative people and distractions, you ultimately determine whether you will remain solution-oriented or be a part of the problem. Recognize that the latter approach is a sure way to ensure you get left behind or to hinder your own career advancement. Always remember that sustainable success requires self-discipline. That first invitation to that important planning meeting will not just fall in your lap. You must be prepared to earn it. Do not sit back and expect that the right energy will always flow. Sometimes, you will need to be prepared to create it. This is your life, so it is up to you to take control. The habit of preparation and adopting a proactive approach in anticipation for when opportunities come your way will prove to be a valuable growth strategy. Acting like you already belong in the room while remaining assertive in your contributions will challenge you to always find creative ways to continually add meaningful value.

Maintaining high personal standards while remaining my true, authentic self has been one of my most gratifying accomplishments. Undoubtedly, you too will be presented with many challenges as you seek to pursue a meaningful and fulfilling career. The ability to positively embrace and grow through these challenges while shaping your personal brand will prove to be a career winning strategy that will raise your profile.

We all have the potential to be the pioneer of our own future. *Life Lessons: A Purpose-Driven Leadership Journey* is my personal testament that it does not matter where you start if you know where you are headed and remain committed to your purpose.

I sincerely thank you for taking the time to read my book. My only hope is that I was able to impart some invaluable insights that will cause you to pause and reflect on your own journey, in pursuit of your God given purpose, potential, and passions.

Life Lessons Summary

"I never forgot where I came from, I just couldn't stay there! You too can be the pioneer of your future."

1. It really does not matter where you start. Once you have a strong purpose, humility, and willpower, you can succeed.

2. Adopting a positive attitude is your new superpower and will without a doubt help you to stand out from amongst your peers.

3. You must be prepared to get up, get dressed, and show up! Showing consistency in your personal qualities and work ethics will improve your individual value and contribution over time.

4. Your personal brand is your career trademark: a collective profile that highlights who you are to others. You get to control what the narrative will say.

5. Be the CEO of your life! Do not leave your career progress to chance. This means you must have a game plan for where you see your future self.

6. It is proven time and time again that what you appreciate, appreciates! Embracing an attitude of gratitude will see you creating greater value while repositioning the way you see things, do things and achieve things.

7. Be prepared to put in the work more, even when you don't feel like it! This can only be achieved with strong discipline in your routine.

8. Accepting accountability is a career winning strategy and a great trademark to have.

9. There is always value in thinking through multiple scenarios but, in the end, you must have the confidence to take decisive action, including taking the risk.

10. Obstacles are just that! There is always a way through to the other side. Just know that if it is really worth it, you will find a way.

11. Always come prepared to overdeliver as that is the best way to truly build capacity and secure your seat at the table.

12. Adopting a growth mindset helps you to better embrace the challenges presented throughout life's journey while helping you to build greater capacity.

13. All feedback should be considered good feedback; but be mindful not to be too quick to take feedback that comes from persons that clearly aren't going anywhere.

14. Be intentional about your level of contribution and efforts to gain a seat at the table.

15. Your overall performance and leadership effectiveness will be very much dependent on your commitment to continuous learning.

16. The law of return in leadership is all about reaching back and helping others once you have reached a certain level of success.

17. Leadership is a complex journey that requires genuine care for others, commitment to ongoing learning, and being prepared to take decisive action when it is needed most.

18. Leading in a crisis will require you to remain calm, be even more connected and be calculating in your strategic decisions and actions.

19. You must constantly seek to strike a balance between saving the world and saving yourself. Remember the power of pause.

20. There really is no end state in sight! Success requires that you are prepared to keep evolving while embracing every new level of the journey towards self-actualization.